The Anti-Corruption Handbook

The Anti-Corruption Handbook

How to Protect Your Business in the Global Marketplace

WILLIAM P. OLSEN

John Wiley & Sons, Inc.

Library of Congress Cataloging-in-Publication Data:

Olsen, William P.
   The anti-corruption handbook : how to protect your business in the global marketplace/William P. Olsen.
     p. cm.
   Includes index.
   ISBN 978-0-470-48450-0 (cloth)
1.   Business ethics–United States. 2.   Corporations–Corrupt practices–United States–Prevention. 3.   Business enterprises–Corrupt practices–United States–Prevention. 4.   Fraud–United States–Prevention. 5.   Compliance auditing.
I. Title.
   HF5387.5.U6O47 2010
   658.4'7–dc22

                                                                    2009044662

To my father, whose integrity was always an inspiration

Contents

Preface

In many parts of the world, companies and governments alike have recognized that corruption raises the risks of doing business. It has a destructive impact on both market opportunities overseas and the broader business climate. Corruption deters foreign investment, stifles economic growth and sustainable development, distorts prices, and undermines legal and judicial systems.

As a result of this growing problem, my colleagues and I wrote this book as a guide to help fight global corruption. We understand the issues and threats that businesses face, and we wanted to provide a comprehensive publication that describes the risks of doing business in the global marketplace and provides precautions that organizations can take to deter such activity. The book also discusses how to respond to allegations of corruption.

Doing business internationally does not need to increase your exposure to fraud and corruption. Whether you are a general counsel, chief financial officer (CFO), internal auditor, compliance officer, forensic accountant—whatever your role or responsibility—we hope that you find this book to be a valuable weapon in the war on corruption. As a U.S. organization trying to operate globally, you need to protect your company's assets and reputation, and run your business successfully and ethically. We want to supply you with the knowledge and tools needed to obtain a competitive advantage in the global markets of the 21st century.

Organization

The book provides background information on anti-corruption and laws and efforts on combating corruption. A basic understanding and foundation is essential in order to effectively prevent, detect, and respond to corruption.

Chapter 1: Managing Corruption Risk
Chapter 2: What is Anti-Corruption?
Chapter 3: U.S. Efforts to Combat Global Corruption

Chapter 4: U.S. Laws Governing Corruption
Chapter 5: The Evolution of the Foreign Corrupt Practices Act
Chapter 6: Internal Controls and Accounting Provisions of FCPA

The book looks closely at certain aspects of the fight against corruption. From governance to whistle-blower programs and information security, we provide details that you should know to protect your organization.

Chapter 7: Do Not Crimp
Chapter 8: The Human Factor
Chapter 9: Corporate
Chapter 10: Whistle-Blower Programs
Chapter 11: Document Retention
Chapter 12: Information Security

There are special areas of anti-corruption that warrant close attention, and these chapters walk you through them.

Chapter 13: Anti–Money Laundering
Chapter 14: Procurement Fraud
Chapter 15: Construction Fraud

So what can you do? Looking at allegations of fraud or the whole playing field overall, there are actions you can take to win the war on corruption.

Chapter 16: Special Investigations
Chapter 17: Navigating the Perils of the Global Marketplace
Chapter 18: Case for Collective Action
Chapter 19: Leveling the Playing Field

How to Use This Book

You can read this book sequentially to gain the necessary background on corruption, learn more details on specific issues and areas of corruption, and then arm yourself with knowledge and advice on how to fight it. Alternatively, you can turn to the chapters covering topics with which you and your business are particularly concerned. This book contains a lot of valuable information at your fingertips and serves as a convenient guide on global corruption.

This book also includes several case studies, tables, charts, and sample work plans to help illustrate the knowledge with practical examples.

Finally, we want you to use the book as a main resource that complements other training and information you receive. While some progress is being achieved globally in this battle, it is an ongoing challenge and a lot of work remains to be done. Add this book to your arsenal to help you and your organization fight the war on corruption.

About the Contributors

William P. Olsen is a principal in the advisory services practice of Grant Thornton LLP and the national practice leader for forensics and investigations. Bill has performed numerous investigations involving management fraud, organized crime, and corruption. He has consulted various organizations in developing policies, controls, and procedures to assure compliance with government regulations. He specializes in the area of anti-corruption and anti–money laundering services.

Dorsey Baskin is a regional partner in charge of professional standards at Grant Thornton LLP, responsible for the central region of the United States. He is consulted on complex accounting, auditing, and risk management matters. In his role, he is directly accessible to engagement teams and available to clients as needed to effectively and timely address matters as they arise.

Danette Edwards is a member of Venable's SEC and White Collar Defense practice group. Her practice is particularly focused on white collar criminal defense, complex civil cases, and corporate compliance and internal control issues, including records management policies and a range of Sarbanes-Oxley–related matters. She also focuses on environmental criminal defense and internal investigations.

Trent Gazzaway is the National Audit Practice Leader and the partner in charge of public policy and corporate governance for Grant Thornton LLP. He collaborates with members of Congress, regulators, and key policy groups to shape policy affecting the accounting profession, investors, businesses, and the global capital markets. He also is a key resource in training Grant Thornton personnel to audit internal controls over financial reporting in accordance with newly established auditing standards.

Kelly Gentenaar is a senior manager in the advisory services practice of Grant Thornton LLP. Kelly has conducted and managed numerous Foreign

Corrupt Practices Act (FCPA) investigations and compliance reviews, as well as forensic accounting investigations. Her experience also includes anti–money laundering investigations and background investigations.

Sterl Greenhalgh is a principal in the London, England, office of Grant Thornton UK. He has focused on international investigations, customs violations, global corruption, and serious fraud. He is a frequent speaker on various subjects involving corruption and FCPA matters.

Nancy R. Grunberg is the head of Venable's Securities and Exchange Commission (SEC) and White Collar Defense practice group. She focuses her practice on securities law and financial disclosure matters. Nancy helps clients address and resolve situations when there may be financial fraud, securities violations, accounting manipulation, or other financial wrongdoing.

Bryan Moser is a director in the advisory services practice of Grant Thornton LLP. Bryan has assisted clients for more than 15 years with a variety of investigations and forensic accounting matters. Client issues have included earnings management, employee embezzlement, improper vendor arrangements, tax evasion using offshore entities, misappropriation of grant and other government funding, and compliance with governmental policies.

Dr. Djordjija Petkoski is a lead enterprise structuring specialist and head of private sector development at the World Bank Institute. Since joining the bank, he has worked in Europe, Asia, Latin America, and Africa. Djordjija has authored or coauthored 15 books and more than 120 articles and has delivered lectures at leading universities and international organizations around the world.

Brad Preber is a partner in the advisory services of Grant Thornton LLP. Brad oversees forensics, investigations, and litigation services provided in the western United States and is the office managing partner of the Phoenix office. He has more than 25 years of experience serving as a litigation consultant, expert witness, forensic accountant, and fraud investigator. He specializes in complex claims and events, with a particular emphasis on class actions, commercial disputes, and fraud claims.

Sri Ramamoorti is a corporate governance consultant and thought leader. He has advised on Sarbanes-Oxley, professional standards, and other technical matters, and contributed to professional development programs. He has published extensively in research and professional journals and is a frequent speaker at academic and professional conferences.

James Schmid is the national construction advisory practice leader for Grant Thornton LLP. He is the practice leader in the Detroit area for forensics, investigations, and litigation. Jim provides economic and damage analysis as an expert witness and litigation support consultant. He also provides fraud investigation services for property and financial statement fraud.

R. Kirt West is the assistant inspector general for Iraq reconstruction. His 20+-year career includes roles such as inspector general of a D.C. not-for-profit organization, assistant inspector general for investigations for the United States Postal Service, and inspector general counsel at the Central Intelligence Agency and the Department of Labor. Kirt has an extensive background in investigating pension fraud, money laundering, contract fraud, false claims, bribery, and criminal conflicts of interest.

CHAPTER 1

Managing Corruption Risk

William P. Olsen

I magine that you are the chief financial officer (CFO) of a Global 1000 company. You are a large and quickly growing company with worldwide operations. Recognizing the risks inherent in conducting business on a global scale, you previously instituted various controls to minimize risks due to unethical and illegal business practices. In spite of this, some concerns have now been raised about the integrity of management at your Latin American operation. In response, you initiate a special investigation to look into the matter. The findings are shocking.

In the course of a few short days, you discover that, despite the controls you installed, a legal minefield of unethical business practices has been uncovered. Over the course of the investigation, the investigative auditors have uncovered a scheme between local management and outside agents to bribe employees of competitors to obtain their proprietary information. They also uncovered a scheme whereby payments were made to government officials overseeing a bid that your company was participating in. The investigation also uncovers evidence of massive vendor kickbacks as well as substantial conflicts of interest in your subsidiary's business dealings. If that is not enough, it is also discovered that the organization was infiltrated by individuals with close ties to organized crime. You now have two questions: (1) how did this happen?, and (2) how can I prevent it from happening again?

The scenario you have just read is based on an actual investigation. As one can see, virtually every element of business corruption was uncovered. The fact that these events took place despite the existence of a corporate code of conduct underscores the need for ongoing monitoring and auditing to assure adherence to the policies and procedures included in the code of conduct and ethics program. In fact, if a program that required proper compliance monitoring had been instituted, the investigation described in the foregoing scenario could have been avoided and the illegal activity certainly would have been discovered earlier.

You Are Not Alone

A recent survey performed by a global business consulting firm discovered that only 50 percent of senior corporate executives are "highly confident" that business control systems are managing their organizations' business risks effectively.

The survey also revealed that fewer than 10 percent of these senior executives rated their control systems as "excellent" in providing early warning signs to catastrophic risks. In an increasingly competitive global marketplace, this could mean trouble for U.S. businesses competing on an uneven international playing field, where foreign competition does not have to adhere to such laws as the Foreign Corrupt Practices Act (FCPA). In fact, there are still many countries that allow "grease payments" as business tax deductions. In addition, there are several other federal initiatives that highlight other areas in which U.S. corporations must address compliance risks.

Bribery and Kickbacks

The greatest threat of business corruption to U.S. companies exists in the emerging markets and developing countries. Corruption and cronyism can have a paralyzing effect on a developing country. The FCPA was adopted in response to scandals involving bribery of foreign officials by U.S. multinational corporations. The FCPA makes it a crime for any U.S. entity or individual to obtain or retain business by paying bribes to foreign government officials. Until recently, the United States was alone in prohibiting such actions. However, groups such as the Organization for Economic Cooperation and Development (OECD) have become more involved in the fight against corruption. In fact, the OECD Convention on Combating Bribery of Foreign Public Officials in International Business Transactions has had the effect of causing many more countries to have criminalized improper payments made to public officials. However, U.S. organizations cannot expect government agencies or international organizations to protect their interests. It is up to the private sector to set the tone and create an environment for integrity.

Economic Espionage

The Economic Espionage Act criminalizes the unauthorized use, access, copying, purchase, sale, and theft of trade secrets, so long as the owner took reasonable steps to protect them. An effective compliance program coupled with sound procedures that are routinely monitored and updated is the most effective tool to limit an organization's potential liability under the act and also an important first step in protecting proprietary information. Organizations must protect against the illicit outflow of their own information as well as the inflow of information from their competitors.

Money Laundering

In an effort to crack down on money laundering transactions, since 9/11 the federal government has enacted new reporting regulations for the banking and financial industry and is planning to extend such regulations to cover money brokers and other businesses and organizations involved in the transfer of large sums of money. The "Suspicious Activity Report" requires financial institutions and other businesses that transfer large amounts of cash to report patterns of suspicious activity by customers. New proposed regulations also call for the development of "Customer Identification Programs," which call for financial institutions to establish procedures and adopt steps to reduce the risk of money laundering under the Bank Secrecy Act, Patriot Act, and other anti–money laundering laws. If implemented correctly, these preventive measures should help financial institutions prevent and detect illegal activity being perpetrated against their organization. It will also assist them in complying with government regulations.

Developing Effective Compliance Programs

These federal initiatives, along with the Sentencing Guidelines for Organizations, have applied increased pressure on all U.S. organizations to develop effective business ethics and anti-corruption programs. The problem, as illustrated at the outset of this chapter, is that many organizations have a false sense of security from current programs that are inadequate.

In the event of a potential violation, the existence of an effective compliance program has proved to be effective in fending off further government inquiry. An effective anti-corruption program must have the foundation of a strong code of conduct that communicates the organization's position on conflicts of interest, bribery, kickbacks, confidentiality of proprietary information, and compliance with all applicable laws and regulations. To be effective, the program must have the support and oversight of top management. The communication of the organization's policies and procedures is also critical in this type of program. Employees need to be constantly apprised of industry trends and new regulations through ongoing training programs.

Once a program is in place, ongoing monitoring is essential. This will not only ensure adherence to established policies and procedures, but will also help prevent fraudulent activity and detect patterns typical of money laundering and other suspicious or corrupt activity when it occurs. Auditors should look for strange or unusual patterns and vary their audit approach so as not to become predictable. The use of exception reporting audit software is becoming a basic tool utilized by auditors to detect patterns of suspicious activity.

Performing Due Diligence

Auditors should utilize a risk-based approach when preparing their audit plans. They should be able to identify the "red flags" of fraud and plan their audit tests accordingly. Companies doing business in countries that are havens for money laundering operations or where bribery and kickbacks are accepted business practice should be extra vigilant.

The performance of background checks to screen key employees, customers, agents, potential partners, and vendors is also an effective tool to identify conflicts of interests, identify government officials, and deter fraudulent activity. What better way to assess the risk of a merger or acquisition than to review the business history of the company and its principal officers for indicators of fraudulent activity, bankruptcy, pending litigation, or even ties to organized crime. Vendor and consulting contracts should point out clearly the organization's expectation that they adhere to all company policies and procedures with regard to business ethics. A "right to audit clause" in the contracts can be a valuable tool if there are ever any allegations of wrongdoing.

Many organizations provide an "ethics hotline" for employees to report suspicions of illegal or unethical activity. If this type of activity becomes apparent, an organization must be prepared to investigate each allegation or suspicion of fraud and take the appropriate action based on results of the investigation.

In summary, the benefits of an effective anti-corruption program are unmistakable: a reduction in the risk of fraud; mitigation of fines and penalties; increased control over business risks; and peace of mind in an increasingly competitive global marketplace.

CHAPTER 2

What Is Anti-Corruption?

William P. Olsen

Corruption has a corrosive impact on both overseas market opportunities and the broader business climate. It also deters foreign investment, stifles economic growth and sustainable development, distorts prices, and undermines legal and judicial systems. More specifically, corruption is a problem in international business transactions, economic development projects, and government procurement activities.

As a result of this problem, and to obtain a competitive advantage in the global markets of the 21st century, a growing number of businesses are taking proactive steps to detect and prevent corruption.

Anti-Corruption Detection and Prevention

Since the Foreign Corrupt Practices Act (FCPA) was enacted in 1977, U.S. law has prohibited offers, promises, or payments to foreign officials, political parties, political officials, and candidates to secure business. A company running afoul of the FCPA, or recently enacted anti-corruption laws of other countries, may subject itself to criminal charges and substantial fines.

Companies in these situations may also face loss of financing and insurance from national or international institutions and debarment from public contracting. Companies committing FCPA violations may also sustain damage to their reputations and their ability to compete for international business. The financial losses incurred due to the loss in reputation can be far more costly than the fine and penalties leveled against companies for FCPA violations.

Developing a comprehensive "anti-corruption" compliance program as part of your company's standard business practice—and that of your foreign subsidiaries—may limit your company's risk and help avoid potential costs.

An anti-corruption compliance strategy can also help to protect your company's reputation, minimize its liability, and maintain its long-term viability.

Critical Elements of an Effective Compliance Program

An effective corporate compliance program, according to the U.S. State Department, is one that ultimately yields intended results: education, detection, and deterrence.

In structuring your corporate compliance program, you may want to consider the following general elements typically found in successful compliance programs. The Federal Sentencing Guidelines for Organizations that were established in 1991 are the benchmark that most organizations utilize to develop compliance programs. The following steps are critical to a successful program.

Tone from the Top

- It is crucial that all of the elements of your company's corporate compliance program receive the full support of upper management.
  - The corporate compliance program must be enforced at all levels within the company.
  - If upper-level management does not take efforts to combat corruption seriously, then neither will employees.

Code of Conduct

- Corporate directors, officers, employees, and agents put themselves at risk of incurring criminal or civil liability when they do not adhere to the FCPA or similar anti-corruption laws of other countries.
  - A corporate code of conduct generally consists of a clearly written set of legal and ethical guidelines for employees to follow.
  - A comprehensive and clearly articulated code of conduct, as well as clear policies and procedures relative to seeking guidance and making disclosures, may reduce the likelihood of actionable misconduct by your employees.
  - It is important that a company's code of conduct be distributed to everyone in the company and, if necessary, translated into the languages of the countries abroad where your company operates.
  - Finally, developing a code of conduct should not be the final act. The code must be effectively implemented and enforced at all times.

Compliance Monitoring

- A compliance program may be run by one person or a team of compliance or ethics officers, depending on the size of your business.

- Implementation and responsibility for a corporate compliance program by high-level management employees are vital for accountability.
- Corporate compliance officers and committees can play key roles in drafting codes of conduct and educating and training employees on compliance procedures. Committee compliance members may include senior vice presidents for marketing and sales, auditing, operations, human resources, and other key offices.
- Past experience has shown that empowering compliance officers with access to senior members of management and with the capacity to influence overall company policy on integrity issues can be of utmost importance.

Training and Communication

- The overall success of a compliance program depends on promoting legal and ethics training at every level of the company.
  - Regular ethics and compliance training programs should be held for all company employees, including board members and senior management officials.
  - Compliance programs should educate employees at all levels of the company about the FCPA and, when necessary, other countries' anticorruption laws.
  - More specific legal and ethical training may be necessary for employees in high-risk areas.
  - A company should also take reasonable measures to communicate its values and procedures in an open environment to encourage participation and feedback.
  - Employees should be informed as to whom they should contact to report violations or ask questions.
  - Training materials that are both interactive and cost effective can help build employee support for a compliance program.
  - Most importantly, compliance issues should not be limited to training classes and the compliance team: compliance should be stressed as an integral part of the company's way of doing business.

Due Diligence

- Conducting prompt and thorough due diligence reviews is vital for ensuring that a compliance program is efficient and effective. Due diligence reviews are also key for preventing potential harm to the company's reputation.
  - Self-monitoring, monitoring of suppliers, government relations consultants, and reports to the board of directors are all good tools for

ensuring that a compliance program is being followed. Moreover, from vetting new hires, agents, or business partners to assessing risks in international business dealings (e.g., mergers, acquisitions, or joint ventures), due diligence reviews can uncover questionable conduct and limit liability.

Auditing and Internal Controls

- Auditing and monitoring of systems of internal accounting controls contribute to building an effective compliance program by the early detection of inaccuracies and misconduct (e.g., bribery, fraud, or other corporate malfeasance). Financial disclosure and reporting should be an integral part of a company's internal accounting controls.
- Companies should have a clear and concise accounting policy that prohibits off-the-books accounts or inadequately identified transactions.
- Companies should monitor their accounts for inaccuracies and for ambiguous or deceptive bookkeeping entries that may disguise illegal bribery payments made by or on behalf of a company. The FCPA requires compliance with various accounting and record-keeping provisions.

We will talk more about accounting controls in Chapter 6.

Reporting Mechanism

- Enforcement of a company's code of conduct is critical. Compliance officers should be accessible so that employees will feel comfortable discussing any of their compliance questions or concerns.
  - Creating reporting mechanisms with adequate policies on confidentiality and nonretaliation, as well as other safeguards related to reporting, is extremely important.
  - Whistle-blowing protections, confidential reporting mechanisms, and "hotlines" facilitate detection and reporting of questionable conduct.
  - Companies should provide guidance to assist employees and agents on how to cope with and resolve difficult situations. Such counseling not only protects the person in the field, it also protects the company.

We will discuss whistle-blower programs more in Chapter 10.

Appropiate Response

- A company should ensure that all employees understand that failure to comply with its compliance policy and procedures will result in disciplinary action, ranging from minor sanctions to more severe punishment, including termination of employment.

- In instances of noncompliance, a company should take the necessary preventive steps to ensure that the questionable conduct does not recur in the future.

The measures listed here are general elements for developing an anti-corruption corporate compliance program. Note that compliance programs' emphasis on specific elements will vary from one company to another, depending on the particular risks engendered by the company's business (e.g., antitrust, health care fraud, construction fraud, or environmental issues). You should seek the advice of legal counsel to learn more about what kind of corporate compliance program is most appropriate for your business.

Governance and Oversight

The emphasis on good governance is timely. Globalization has put a premium on developing the incentives and adjustments necessary to attract investments and capital in foreign markets.

You are the most effective advocate in the fight against corruption because you play a part in controlling jobs and investment in the global economy. Good governance starts with a culture of integrity. Culture comes down from the top.

Good corporate governance procedures provide fair, reliable, and transparent rules that foster trust and confidence for doing business. As corporate citizens, businesspeople are members of and leaders in their communities. Your efforts to establish and adhere to corporate codes of conduct and personal ethical standards have a beneficial effect that ripples through the community. By working with governments and civil society to promote good governance in global economies, your company will help foster a synergy between economic goals and social progress.

Good governance principles for governments also benefit their economies. Good governance reduces market volatility, encourages foreign direct investment and capital inflows, promotes sustainable economic growth, and produces a more equitable distribution of resources to the people and creates an atmosphere of fair competition in the marketplace.

While it is increasingly clear that corporate governance and sound business practices are generally good for business, good governance practices by governments also enhance the integrity of the international markets and promote the integration of economies into the global trading system.

Thus, governments and businesses alike have a mutual interest in working together to strengthen public-private governance practices that promote and reward efficiency, innovation, and openness. Moreover, public and corporate governance principles are also important in nurturing the investment climate and building a more democratic rule of law-based society.

As you conduct your business overseas, or if you are considering entering a new foreign market, let foreign government officials and business partners know that anti-corruption and good governance policies will help their economy—and your company—sustain long-term investment and growth.

The Organization for Economic Cooperation and Development (OECD) recommends that government policies such as the following, which emphasize transparency, due process, and accountability, make for a strong anti-corruption environment:

- Commercial codes that provide protection for international contracts as well as effective dispute settlement and arbitration methods.
- Law enforcement and judicial procedures that promote due process and the rule of law.
- Independent systems to promote and ensure the integrity and efficiency of governmental agencies.
- Civil service reforms and competitive wages for government employees.
- Integrity of capital markets and financial disclosure on the issuance of securities.
- Predictable and transparent administrative and bidding processes in areas such as procurement and privatization.
- Improved and standardized public accounting, auditing, and management systems.
- Effective bankruptcy and insolvency laws.
- Limits on discretionary authority for officials who perform inspections or audits, oversee procurement, grant licenses and permits, or provide final approval for contracts or projects.
- Oversight mechanisms and appellate remedies to challenge arbitrary or unlawful actions.
- Protection for whistle-blowers and the media.
- Disclosure of and access to public records and information.
- Encouragement of civil society's participation in implementing these policies and anti-corruption efforts.

We will talk more about working with government when we discuss the World Bank collective action program. Bringing government, industry, and civil society together to combat corruption is an essential element to the success of any anti-corruption program.

CHAPTER 3

U.S. Efforts to Combat Global Corruption

William P. Olsen

B usiness thrives on competition. U.S. companies and workers can compete with the best in the global marketplace because of their drive, innovation, and quality products and services. However, their success depends heavily on their ability to compete on a level playing field. Bribery and corruption tilt the playing field and create unfair advantages for those willing to engage in unethical or illegal behavior. Corrupt practices penalize companies that play fair and seek to win contracts through the quality and price of their products and services.

Since the enactment of the Foreign Corrupt Practices Act (FCPA), the United States has been trying to level the playing field by encouraging other industrialized countries to take similar steps—and these efforts are finally paying off. There has been real progress in building an international coalition to fight bribery and public corruption so that all businesses may fairly compete in the global marketplace.

One significant milestone is the Organization for Economic Cooperation and Development's (OECD's) Convention on Combating Bribery of Foreign Public Officials in International Business Transactions, commonly known as the OECD Bribery Convention, which entered into force in February 1999. The OECD Bribery Convention, originally signed by 34 countries, marks a sea change in the fight against corruption by obligating its parties to criminalize the bribery of foreign public officials in the conduct of international business.

The OECD Bribery Convention also requires parties to apply "effective, proportionate, and dissuasive criminal penalties" to those who bribe; establish liability of "legal persons" (i.e., corporations, partnerships, and similar business entities) or impose comparable civil sanctions or fines; make bribery a predicate offense for money laundering legislation; improve accounting procedures; prohibit off-the-books accounts; and provide mutual legal assistance and extradition in cases falling under the Convention.

The U.S. Department of Commerce lists the following as key goals of the U.S. anti-corruption policy:

- Full ratification, implementation, and enforcement of the OECD Bribery Convention by all signatories.
- Full ratification, implementation, and enforcement of the Inter-American Convention against Corruption by all hemispheric partners.
- Nurture stability in democratic institutions and strengthen the rule of law in transitional economies.
- Promote global and regional anti-corruption norms and initiatives that deter and punish corruption.
- Ensure transparency in government procurement procedures to enhance openness, disclosure, and predictability.
- Develop ethical and administrative codes of conduct that promote the highest levels of professionalism and integrity in government.
- Engage the business community to join the United States and other governments in promoting corporate governance, transparency, and integrity in business operations.
- Foster an active civil society that is involved in participatory governance and upholds democratic principles.

The Emergence of Nongovernment Organizations

The U.S. Department of State recently stated that many international organizations have been making strides in addressing international bribery in business transactions, official public corruption, and transparency issues.

These initiatives represent important steps in building coalitions to combat corruption. For more than a decade, the U.S. government has worked cooperatively with the private sector and international organizations on these and other anti-corruption initiatives.

U.S. and international legal, business, and accounting associations and nongovernmental organizations (NGOs)—such as the American Bar Association (ABA), the U.S. Chamber of Commerce, the International Chamber of Commerce (ICC), the Ethics Officer Association (EOA), the Committee of Sponsoring Organizations of the Treadway Commission (COSO), and Transparency International (TI)—have played key advisory roles in the development of various anti-corruption initiatives.

With respect to the emerging international anti-corruption environment, the unifying concept in all of the global and regional processes is that effective action to prevent, detect, and punish corruption must be taken by each individual government. The international community can advance this process by raising the visibility and political profile of these efforts.

The international business community and NGOs are working together to identify clear and objective actions of what should be expected of governments; what governments may expect of each other; and what their citizens, through democratic processes, ultimately should require of their governments.

In working with other nations, the United States continues to encourage a broad range of global and regional anti-corruption and transparency initiatives. Such measures strengthen the political will for cooperation on building capacities for action against corruption and for developing effective measures and practices to promote public integrity.

World Trade Organization

Through binding commitments to ensure transparency and due process in a wide range of government activities relating to international trade, the World Trade Organization (WTO) makes an important contribution to international efforts to combat bribery and corruption. Most WTO members have endorsed efforts to conclude a multilateral agreement on transparency in government procurement, under which all 140 members would make binding international commitments to ensure transparency and predictability in their government procurement procedures. Similarly, an initiative on trade facilitation would help eliminate irregularities in WTO members' customs regimes, another area of economic activity that is frequently susceptible to corrupt practices.

Global Forum on Fighting Corruption

The First Global Forum on Fighting Corruption and Safeguarding Integrity, hosted by the United States in February 1999, added momentum to broader anti-corruption campaign. Participants from 90 governments agreed to a final conference declaration, calling on governments to adopt principles and effective practices to fight corruption, to promote transparency and good governance, and to create ways to assist each other through mutual evaluation.

The First Global Forum identified a set of 12 Guiding Principles that encompass the goals or purposes that a national anti-corruption effort must address. These Guiding Principles include aspects relating to:

- Laws prohibiting the full range of corruption offenses, with sanctions and remedies sufficient to deter corrupt activities.
- Investigative and enforcement institutions with the impartiality, powers, and resources to detect, investigate, and prosecute violations of those laws.
- Codes of conduct, public management, and personnel measures and procedures that promote the integrity of public officials.
- Freedom of the media and public to receive and impart information on corruption matters and to bring complaints of suspected corruption.
- Enhanced research and public discussion of all aspects of upholding integrity and preventing corruption among public officials.
- International cooperation in all aspects of this issue.

The most fundamental conclusion from the First Global Forum is that action against corruption must encompass all political, administrative, judicial, and civil society elements of a nation. National anti-corruption actions must comprehensively respond to all aspects of these Guiding Principles if they are to succeed. These principles have become the foundation for many international initiatives to combat corruption.

International Financial Institutions

The World Bank, Inter-American Development Bank, and the International Monetary Fund (IMF) have determined that corruption is a serious deterrent to economic growth and financial stability and must be addressed in the context of economic and financial evaluations and assistance programs. The World Bank and the regional development banks, especially in Asia and Africa, have established explicit anti-corruption policies aimed at helping countries to confront and prevent corruption through appropriate economic and civil service reforms.

All of the official development banks, led by the World Bank, are working together to agree on standard procurement bidding documents and rules to ensure fairness to all competing suppliers and efficiency in the use of public sector funds. The continued involvement of the development banks in combating corruption will be critical to a successful effort.

The IMF has begun to integrate identification of corruption problems into its standard evaluations. In selected cases, the IMF and the World Bank have postponed, denied, or suspended assistance to countries where endemic corruption was adversely affecting financial stabilization or development programs and where governments were not prepared to acknowledge and deal with those problems.

International Chamber of Commerce

The ICC, the world business organization, promotes an open international trade and investment system and the market economy. The ICC makes model rules to govern the conduct of business across borders. In 1977, the ICC issued "Rules of Conduct to Combat Extortion and Bribery." The rules were revised in 1996, and the ICC reissued them unchanged in 1999. In the spring of 1999, the ICC also published a manual of best corporate practices to accompany the rules of conduct and to provide guidance for compliance with the OECD Bribery Convention. The ICC rules, which promote integrity in business transactions, are intended as a method of self-regulation by international business.

Transparency International

TI is a nonprofit advocacy organization working to curb corruption in international business transactions and other areas. Through its national chapters in over 80 countries, TI encourages national and local governments to implement effective anti-corruption laws, policies, and programs. TI serves as secretariat for the biennial International Anti-Corruption Conference (IACC) that brings together practitioners and academics to exchange information and ideas about the fight against corruption. TI also works at the multilateral level with the World Bank, IMF, Organization of American States (OAS), OECD, Asia-Pacific Economic Cooperation (APEC), Global Coalition for Africa (GCA), and other public organizations. The annual TI Corruption Perceptions Index, which reflects perceived levels of corruption in foreign countries, continues to generate widespread attention. TI has also launched a Bribe Payers Index, which ranks leading exporting countries in terms of the degree to which their corporations are perceived to be paying bribes abroad. Take a look at the countries listed at the top of the bribe payer's index and compare it to countries that are listed at the top of the emerging markets. You will see a lot of the same countries on both lists.

Global Corporate Governance Forum

The World Bank and OECD launched the Global Corporate Governance Forum, which aims to promote and improve corporate governance on a worldwide basis. Among the lessons learned in recent and past international financial crises is that good corporate governance is an essential foundation for a well-functioning market economy, for enhancing individual countries' long-term economic performance, and for strengthening the international financial system. The Global Corporate Governance Forum provides a framework for international cooperation and for creating synergies for the design and implementation of joint or individual projects by participating countries and institutions.

Through complementary OECD–World Bank regional roundtables, the initiative brings together leaders from government, private sector, international financial institutions, international organizations, NGOs, and other stakeholders to foster cooperation on identifying key areas for technical assistance, developing effective corporate governance systems, and helping create the necessary legal and regulatory infrastructure to support them.

The Role of Civil Society

According to the U.S. State Department, the hallmark of a free society is the ability of individuals to associate with other like-minded citizens, associations, and organizations; express their views; petition their governments; and accept the rule of law.

The role of civil society as a catalyst for fighting corruption and mobilizing pressure on governments and multilateral governmental organizations to adopt public sector reforms cannot be underestimated.

In many parts of the world, business is partnering with civil society to prevent corrupt practices, strengthen public institutions, and foster an anti-corruption culture in society.

The U.S. government continues to work toward and support the creation of a viable civil society where it does not exist and to strengthen the capacity and opportunity of public-private partnerships to fight corruption. The U.S. State Department usually refers to the term *civil society* as diverse citizen associations and NGOs that unite to promote causes or issues of mutual interest and to influence decision-making processes. These include, for example, professional associations, civic education groups, religious organizations, bar associations, business councils and labor federations, human rights and women's rights groups, journalists and the media, and other monitoring groups and organizations.

The Emerging Markets

The fight against corruption remains among the most significant international issues; however, a lot of work remains to be done. While some progress is being achieved globally in this battle, new challenges arise each day.

The BRIC countries (Brazil, Russia, India, China), though increasingly considered together as a global force for change, are in fact a diverse group. Both mainland China and India have populations of over 1 billion each.

Historically, they were the largest economies in the world before the industrialization of North America, western Europe, and Japan. These vastly different political and economic histories have helped shape current developments and attitudes. The impetus for growth stems mainly from manufacturing in mainland China, while India's growth is boosted by software services and call centers. Mainland China can already claim to be a global economic superpower, and India looks set to follow suit in the next few decades.

Brazil and Russia have much smaller populations: 186 million in Brazil (rising strongly) and 142 million in Russia (declining steadily). In Brazil, exploitation of raw materials is the key driver of economic growth, but the industrial sector is developing strongly, led by machinery and transport equipment. In Russia, the exploitation of energy resources underpins the vibrant economic growth of recent years.

The next generation? While the four emerging market BRIC economies are having huge impacts on the global economy, there are other countries waiting in the wings to follow suit. Indonesia, Mexico, Pakistan, and Turkey appear to be contesting the fight to become the next major emerging economy.

There are many differences among Indonesia, Mexico, Pakistan, and Turkey, some of which have yet to take off, while others are well on the way to industrial modernization. Yet they are all large economies that can have a significant influence on the global market, provided that issues such as sociopolitical problems can be overcome. While these countries are not in the same league as mainland China and India, they certainly have the potential to rival Brazil and Russia in terms of economic clout in coming years.

Indonesia and Pakistan, with their large populations, have the potential to grow through labor-intensive exports and could capitalize on the process of low-cost production that mainland China has so successfully exploited. Mexico is benefiting from its close trading ties with the rest of North American through the North America Free Trade Agreement (NAFTA) and is well placed to play a more significant role in the Americas. Turkey is expanding robustly and is on the path to making the transition to a modern industrial economy; it is set to increase its influence in western Europe and the Middle East.

While the BRIC economies lead the emerging markets, opportunities are evident for others to seize the opportunity. Opportunity often opens the door to corruption if countries and organizations are not prepared to manage the risk.

In many regions, the public outcry against corruption has influenced the outcome of elections. Corruption has also been a factor in global financial crises and continues to be an impediment to trade liberalization and sustainable development. Perhaps the most pernicious effect of corruption is when it undermines the fragile institutions that safeguard democracy and foster market economies.

The lessons learned from the international community's collective governance experiences and hardships present a compelling case that corrupt practices and the erosion of integrity not only destabilize economies and democratic institutions, but also directly and adversely impact those who stand to benefit the most from good governance. As a recent World Bank study illustrates, good governance helps achieve a better quality of economic growth for countries around the world. This is particularly true in countries that have efficient markets and strong oversight institutions, where the rule of law is enforced and where civil society has a voice and actively participates in sustainable development.

Because corruption knows no national boundaries, the international community must engage in strategic planning and coordinate transnational approaches. A global consensus is emerging that governance and anti-corruption capacity building must incorporate a more holistic approach that focuses on comprehensively integrating checks and balances, preventive measures, internal controls, effective law enforcement, education awareness campaigns, and public-private partnerships. The rule of law must be reinforced by the dynamic and participatory democratic activities of business, civil society, and NGO groups. The media also must have an unfettered voice in this process.

Working together, the international community can develop a more stable and predictable investment climate by reducing the level of corruption. A strong anti-corruption regime and good governance practices allow decision makers in both the private and public sectors to limit their financial risks, develop effective warning systems, nurture long-term growth, and minimize future economic and political destabilization situations.

CHAPTER 4

U.S. Laws Governing Corruption

William P. Olsen

A side from the Foreign Corrupt Practices Act (FCPA), there are many other laws and regulations that address the problem of corruption. These laws deal with everything from bribes, kickbacks, price fixing, and bid rigging to intellectual property theft. This chapter covers some of the U.S. laws that govern these areas of corruption.

Racketeer Influenced and Corrupt Organizations Act

The Racketeer Influenced and Corrupt Organizations Act (commonly referred to as the RICO Act or RICO) is a U.S. federal law that provides for extended criminal penalties and a civil cause of action for acts performed as part of an ongoing criminal organization. RICO was enacted by section 901(a) of the Organized Crime Control Act of 1970 (Pub. L. 91-452, 84 Stat. 922, enacted October 15, 1970). RICO is codified as Chapter 96 of Title 18 of the United States Code, 18 U.S.C. §1961–1968. While its intended use was to prosecute those who were actively engaged in organized crime, its application has been more widespread.

Under RICO, a person who is a member of an enterprise that has committed any 2 of 35 crimes—27 federal crimes and 8 state crimes—within a 10-year period can be charged with racketeering. Those found guilty of racketeering can be fined up to $25,000 and/or sentenced to 20 years in prison per racketeering count. In addition, the racketeer must forfeit all ill-gotten gains and interest in any business gained through a pattern of "racketeering activity." RICO also permits a private individual harmed by the actions of such an enterprise to file a civil suit, as discussed further below; if successful, the individual can collect treble damages.

When the U.S. attorney decides to indict someone under RICO, he or she has the option of seeking a pretrial restraining order or injunction to temporarily seize a defendant's assets and prevent the transfer of potentially forfeitable property, as well as require the defendant to put up a performance bond. This provision was placed in the law because the owners of organized crime–related shell corporations often absconded with the assets. An injunction and/or performance bond ensures that there is something to seize in the event of a guilty verdict.

In many cases, the threat of a RICO indictment can force defendants to plead guilty to lesser charges, in part because the seizure of assets would make it difficult to pay a defense attorney. Despite its harsh provisions, a RICO-related charge is considered easy to prove in court, as it focuses on patterns of behavior as opposed to criminal acts.

As stated previously, there is also a provision for private parties to sue. A "person damaged in his business or property" can sue one or more "racketeers." The plaintiff must prove the existence of a "criminal enterprise." The defendant(s) are not the enterprise; in other words, the defendant(s) and the enterprise are not one and the same. There must be one of four specified relationships between the defendant(s) and the enterprise. A civil RICO action, like many lawsuits based on federal law, can be filed in state or federal court.

Both the federal and civil components allow for the recovery of treble damages (damages in triple the amount of actual/compensatory damages).

Although its primary intent was to deal with organized crime, prosecutors and regulators often use this law when piling on the charges in a corruption case. Often, simple collusion is all it takes to make the charges stick.

RICO Offenses

Under the law, racketeering activity means:

- Any violation of state statutes against gambling, murder, kidnapping, arson, robbery, bribery, extortion, dealing in obscene matter, or dealing in a controlled substance or listed chemical (as defined in the Controlled Substances Act).
- Any act of bribery, counterfeiting, theft, embezzlement, fraud, dealing in obscene matter, obstruction of justice, slavery, racketeering, gambling, money laundering, commission of murder for hire, and several other offenses covered under the federal criminal code (Title 18).
- Embezzlement of union funds.
- Bankruptcy or securities fraud.

- Drug trafficking.
- Money laundering and related offenses.
- Bringing in, aiding, or assisting aliens in illegally entering the country (if the action was for financial gain).
- Acts of terrorism.

Violations of the RICO laws can be alleged in cases where civil lawsuits or criminal charges are brought against individuals or corporations in retaliation for said individuals or corporations working with law enforcement, or against individuals or corporations who have sued or filed criminal charges against a defendant.

The late 2000s global recession may force RICO to be used against the U.S. banking and finance system. The reasoning is that finance institutions allegedly have specifically been using their error accounts to engage in racketeering practices. Error accounts in the United States and European finance system are rumored to be in the trillions of dollars, enough to totally annihilate the gross domestic product (GDP) and currencies of the United States, United Kingdom, and euro countries. While euro accounts are perfectly legal under generally accepted accounting principles (GAAP), the use of euro accounts to engage in money laundering and other irregular financial system practices is not.

The U.S. RICO legislation has other equivalents in the rest of the world. In spite of Interpol's having a standardized definition of RICO-like crimes, the interpretation and national implementation in legislation (and enforcement) varies widely. Most nations do cooperate with the United States on RICO enforcement only where their own related laws are specifically broken, but this is in line with the Interpol protocols for such matters.

Sherman Antitrust Act

The Sherman Antitrust Act (18 U.S.C. 201; 1890; criminal amendment of 2004) is often used to prosecute acts of price fixing, bid rigging, and market allocation.

In a free-enterprise system, consumers should be able to expect the best goods and services at the lowest prices. Public and private organizations often rely on a competitive bidding process to achieve that end. The competitive process works, however, only when competitors set prices honestly and independently. When competitors collude, prices are inflated and the customer is cheated. Price fixing, bid rigging, and other forms of collusion are illegal and are subject to criminal prosecution by the Sherman Antitrust Act.

The act prohibits any agreement among competitors to fix prices, rig bids, or engage in other anticompetitive activity. Criminal prosecution of Sherman Act violations is the responsibility of the Antitrust Division of the U.S. Department of Justice.

Violation of the Sherman Act is a felony punishable by a fine of up to $10 million for corporations, and a fine of up to $350,000 or three years' imprisonment (or both) for individuals. In addition, collusion among competitors may constitute violations of the mail or wire fraud statute, the false statements statute, or other federal felony statutes, all of which the Antitrust Division prosecutes.

In addition to receiving a criminal sentence, a corporation or individual convicted of a Sherman Antitrust Act violation may be ordered to make restitution to the victims for all overcharges. Victims of bid-rigging and price-fixing conspiracies also may seek civil recovery of up to three times the amount of damages suffered.

Most criminal antitrust prosecutions involve price fixing, bid rigging, or market division or allocation schemes. Each of these forms of collusion may be prosecuted criminally if they occurred, at least in part, within the past five years. Proving such a crime does not require proof that the conspirators entered into a formal written or express agreement. Price fixing, bid rigging, and other collusive agreements can be established either by direct evidence, such as the testimony of a participant, or by circumstantial evidence, such as suspicious bid patterns, travel and expense reports, telephone records, and business diary entries.

Under the law, price-fixing and bid-rigging schemes are per se violations of the Sherman Act. This means that where such a collusive scheme has been established, it cannot be justified under the law by arguments or evidence that, for example, the agreed-upon prices were reasonable, the agreement was necessary to prevent or eliminate price cutting or ruinous competition, or the conspirators were merely trying to make sure that each got a fair share of the market.

In recent years, the Antitrust Division has successfully prosecuted regional, national, and international conspiracies affecting construction, agricultural products, manufacturing, service industries, consumer products, and many other sectors of the economy. Many of these prosecutions resulted from information uncovered by members of the general public who reported the information to the Antitrust Division.

Anti-Kickback Act of 1986

The Anti-Kickback Act of 1986, 41 U.S.C. §51 et seq., modernized and closed the loopholes of previous statutes applying to government contractors. The

1986 law attempts to make the anti-kickback statute a more useful prosecutorial tool by expanding the definition of prohibited conduct and by making the statute applicable to a broader range of persons involved in government subcontracting. This is another act that prosecutors often use when piling on the charges in a corruption case. Prosecutions under these statutes must establish the following:

- *Prohibited conduct.* The act prohibits attempted as well as completed "kickbacks," which include any money, fees, commission, credit, gift, gratuity, thing of value, or compensation of any kind. The act also provides that the inclusion of kickback amounts in contract prices is prohibited conduct in itself.
- *Purpose of kickback.* The act requires that the purpose of the kickback was for improperly obtaining or rewarding favorable treatment. It is intended to embrace the full range of government contracting. Prior to 1986, the "kickback" was required to be for the inducement or acknowledgment of a subcontract.
- *Covered class of kickback recipients.* The act prohibits kickbacks to prime contractors, prime contractor employees, subcontractors, and subcontractor employees. These terms are defined in the act.
- *Type of contract.* The act defines kickbacks to include payments under any government contract. Prior to this legislation, the statutes' applicability was limited to negotiated contracts.
- *Knowledge and willfulness.* The act requires one to knowingly and willfully engage in the prohibited conduct for the imposition of criminal sanctions.

Economic Espionage Act of 1996

The Economic Espionage Act of 1996 (EEA) (18 U.S.C. §1831–1839) makes the theft or misappropriation of a trade secret a federal crime. Unlike espionage, which is governed by Title 18 U.S. Code Sections 792–799, the offense involves commercial information, not classified or national defense information.

This law contains two sections criminalizing two sorts of activity. The first, 18 U.S.C. §1831(a), criminalizes the misappropriation of trade secrets (including conspiracy to misappropriate trade secrets and the subsequent acquisition of such misappropriated trade secrets) with the knowledge or intent that the theft will benefit a foreign power. Penalties for violation are fines of up to US$500,000 per offense and imprisonment of up to 15 years for individuals, and fines of up to US$10 million for organizations.

The second section, 18 U.S.C. §1832, criminalizes the misappropriation of trade secrets related to or included in a product that is produced for or placed in interstate (including international) commerce, with the knowledge or intent that the misappropriation will injure the owner of the trade secret. Penalties for violation of section 1832 are imprisonment for up to 10 years for individuals (no fines) and fines of up to US$5 million for organizations.

In addition to these specific penalties, section 1834 of the EEA also requires criminal forfeiture of (1) any proceeds of the crime and property derived from proceeds of the crime and (2) any property used, or intended to be used, in commission of the crime.

The act authorizes civil proceedings by the Department of Justice to enjoin violations of the act, but does not create a private cause of action. Thus, victims or putative victims must work with the U.S. attorney in order to obtain an injunction.

The EEA has extraterritorial jurisdiction where:

- The offender is a U.S. citizen or permanent resident; or
- The offender is an organization organized under the laws of the United States or any State or political subdivision thereof; or
- An act in furtherance of the offense was committed in the United States.

Trade secrets are defined in the act consistent with generally accepted legal definitions such as those used in the Uniform Trade Secrets Act (UTSA) and state laws based on the UTSA, to refer broadly to information, whether in tangible or intangible form, that (1) is subject to reasonable measures to preserve its secrecy, and (2) derives independent economic value from its not being generally known to or ascertainable by the public.

This legislation has created much debate within the business intelligence community regarding the legality and ethics of various forms of information gathering designed to provide business decision makers with competitive advantages in areas such as strategy, marketing, research and development, or negotiations. Most business intelligence (also known as competitive intelligence practitioners) rely largely on the collection and analysis of open source information from which they identify events, patterns, and trends of actionable interest. However, some techniques focus on the collection of publicly available information that is in limited circulation. This may be obtained through a number of direct and indirect techniques that share common origins in the national intelligence community. The use of these techniques is often debated from legal and ethical standpoints based on this act.

One such example is the collection and analysis of gray literature. The techniques for developing actionable intelligence from limited circula-tion/limited availability documents such as selected corporate publications can raise difficult legal and ethical questions under both intellectual property laws and the EEA.

The EEA was developed on the basis of a national philosophy that emphasizes a "level playing field" for all business competitors that arose in no small part due to the size and diversity of the American private sector. Many other nations not only lack such legislation, but actively support industrial espionage using both their national intelligence services as well as less formal mechanisms, including bribery and corruption.

CHAPTER 5

The Evolution of the Foreign Corrupt Practices Act

William P. Olsen

The Foreign Corrupt Practices Act (FCPA) has evolved into the mother of all anti-corruption legislation. The law was originally enacted in the post-Watergate era as a response to widespread global corruption that was identified during that time period. The law has had a renaissance in recent years. The Department of Justice (DOJ) has reported a large increase in prosecutions, and that trend appears to be continuing. The act provides stiff penalties for both individuals and organizations, and therefore, it is important to be familiar with the contents of the law.

Background

The 1988 Trade Act directed the attorney general to provide guidance concerning the DOJ's enforcement policy with respect to the FCPA (15 U.S.C. §§78dd-1, et seq.) to potential exporters and small businesses that are unable to obtain specialized counsel on issues related to the FCPA. The guidance is limited to responses to requests under the DOJ's Foreign Corrupt Practices Act Opinion Procedure and to general explanations of compliance responsibilities and potential liabilities under the FCPA. The following information constitutes the DOJ's general explanation of the FCPA. U.S. firms seeking to do business in foreign markets must be familiar with the FCPA. In general, the FCPA prohibits corrupt payments to foreign officials for the purpose of obtaining or keeping business. The DOJ is the chief enforcement agency, with a coordinate role played by the Securities and Exchange Commission (SEC). The Office of General Counsel of the Department of Commerce also answers general questions from U.S. exporters concerning the FCPA's basic requirements and constraints.

As a result of SEC investigations in the mid-1970s, over 400 U.S. companies admitted making questionable or illegal payment in excess of $300 million to foreign government officials, politicians, and political parties. The abuses ran the gamut from bribery of high foreign officials to secure some type of favorable action by a foreign government to so-called facilitating payments that allegedly were made to ensure that government functionaries discharged certain ministerial or clerical duties. Congress enacted the FCPA to bring a halt to the bribery of foreign officials and to restore public confidence in the integrity of the American business system.

The FCPA was intended to have and has had an enormous impact on the way American firms do business. Several firms that paid bribes to foreign officials have been the subject of criminal and civil enforcement actions, resulting in large fines and suspension and debarment from federal procurement contracting, and their employees and officers have gone to jail. To avoid such consequences, many firms have implemented detailed compliance programs intended to prevent and to detect any improper payments by employees and agents.

Following the passage of the FCPA, Congress became concerned that American companies were operating at a disadvantage compared to foreign companies who routinely paid bribes and, in some countries, were permitted to deduct the cost of such bribes as business expenses on their taxes. Accordingly, in 1988, Congress directed the executive branch to commence negotiations in the Organization of Economic Cooperation and Development (OECD) to obtain the agreement of the United States' major trading partners to enact legislation similar to the FCPA. In 1997, almost 10 years later, the United States and 33 other countries signed the OECD Convention on Combating Bribery of Foreign Public Officials in International Business Transactions. The United States ratified this Convention and enacted implementing legislation in 1998.

The anti-bribery provisions of the FCPA make it unlawful for a U.S. person, and certain foreign issuers of securities, to make a corrupt payment to a foreign official for the purpose of obtaining or retaining business for or with, or directing business to, any person. Since 1998, the provisions also apply to foreign firms and persons who take any act in furtherance of such a corrupt payment while in the United States.

The FCPA also requires companies whose securities are listed in the United States to meet its accounting provisions (see 15 U.S.C. §78m). These accounting provisions, which were designed to operate in tandem with the anti-bribery provisions of the FCPA, require corporations covered by the provisions to make and keep books and records that accurately and fairly reflect the transactions of the corporation and to devise and maintain an adequate system of internal accounting controls. The information below discusses only the anti-bribery provisions.

The DOJ is responsible for all criminal enforcement and for civil enforcement of the anti-bribery provisions with respect to domestic concerns and foreign companies and nationals. The SEC is responsible for civil enforcement of the anti-bribery provisions with respect to issuers.

Anti-Bribery Provisions

Basic Prohibitions

The FCPA makes it unlawful to bribe foreign government officials to obtain or retain business. With respect to the basic prohibition, there are five elements that must be met to constitute a violation of the act. These are discussed in this section.

WHO   The FCPA potentially applies to any individual, firm, officer, director, employee, or agent of a firm and any stockholder acting on behalf of a firm. Individuals and firms may also be penalized if they order, authorize, or assist someone else to violate the anti-bribery provisions or if they conspire to violate those provisions.

Under the FCPA, U.S. jurisdiction over corrupt payments to foreign officials depends on whether the violator is an "issuer," a "domestic concern," or a foreign national or business.

An "issuer" is a corporation that has issued securities that have been registered in the United States or that is required to file periodic reports with the SEC.

A "domestic concern" is any individual who is a citizen, national, or resident of the United States, or any corporation, partnership, association, joint-stock company, business trust, unincorporated organization, or sole proprietorship that has its principal place of business in the United States, or that is organized under the laws of a state of the United States, or a territory, possession, or commonwealth of the United States.

Issuers and domestic concerns may be held liable under the FCPA under either territorial or nationality jurisdiction principles. For acts taken within the territory of the United States, issuers and domestic concerns are liable if they take an act in furtherance of a corrupt payment to a foreign official using the U.S. mails or other means or instrumentalities of interstate commerce. Such means of instrumentalities include telephone calls, facsimile transmissions, wire transfers, and interstate or international travel. In addition, issuers and domestic concerns may be held liable for any act in furtherance of a corrupt payment taken outside the United States. Thus, a U.S. company or national may be held liable for a corrupt payment authorized by employees or agents operating entirely outside the United States, using money from foreign bank accounts, and without any involvement by personnel located within the United States.

Prior to 1998, foreign companies, with the exception of those who qualified as "issuers" and foreign nationals were not covered by the FCPA. The 1998 amendments expanded the FCPA to assert territorial jurisdiction over foreign companies and nationals. A foreign company or person is now subject to the FCPA if it causes, directly or through agents, an act in furtherance of the corrupt payment to take place within the territory of the United States. There is, however, no requirement that such act make use of the U.S. mail or other means or instrumentalities of interstate commerce.

Finally, U.S. parent corporations may be held liable for the acts of foreign subsidiaries where they authorized, directed, or controlled the activity in question, as can U.S. citizens or residents, themselves "domestic concerns," who were employed by or acting on behalf of such foreign-incorporated subsidiaries.

CORRUPT INTENT The person making or authorizing the payment must have a corrupt intent, and the payment must be intended to induce the recipient to misuse his or her official position to direct business wrongfully to the payer or to any other person. It should be noted that the FCPA does not require that a corrupt act succeed in its purpose. The offer or promise of a corrupt payment can constitute a violation of the statute. The FCPA prohibits any corrupt payment intended to influence any act or decision of a foreign official in his or her official capacity, to induce the official to do or omit to do any act in violation of his or her lawful duty, to obtain any improper advantage, or to induce a foreign official to use his or her influence improperly to affect or influence any act or decision.

PAYMENT The FCPA prohibits paying, offering, promising to pay (or authorizing to pay or offer) money or anything of value.

RECIPIENT The prohibition extends only to corrupt payments to a foreign official, a foreign political party or party official, or any candidate for foreign political office. A "foreign official" means any officer or employee of a foreign government, a public international organization, or any department or agency thereof, or any person acting in an official capacity.

You should consider utilizing the services of outside legal counsel for particular questions as to the definition of a "foreign official," such as whether a member of a royal family, a member of a legislative body, or an official of a state-owned business enterprise would be considered a foreign official. In addition, you should consult the list of public international organizations covered under the FCPA that is available on the DOJ's FCPA Web site.

The FCPA applies to payments to any public official, regardless of rank or position. The FCPA focuses on the purpose of the payment instead of the particular duties of the official receiving the payment, offer, or promise of payment, and there are exceptions to the anti-bribery provision for "facilitating payments for routine governmental action."

BUSINESS PURPOSE TEST The FCPA prohibits payments made in order to assist the firm in obtaining or retaining business for or with, or directing business to, any person. The DOJ interprets "obtaining or retaining business" broadly, such that the term encompasses more than the mere award or renewal of a contract. It should be noted that the business to be obtained or retained does not need to be with a foreign government or foreign government instrumentality.

Third-Party Payments

The FCPA prohibits corrupt payments through intermediaries. It is unlawful to make a payment to a third party, while knowing that all or a portion of the payment will go directly or indirectly to a foreign official. The term *knowing* includes conscious disregard and deliberative ignorance. The elements of an offense are essentially the same as described above, except that in this case the "recipient" is the intermediary who is making the payment to the requisite "foreign official."

Intermediaries may include joint venture partners or agents. To avoid being liable for corrupt third-party payments, U.S. companies are encouraged to exercise due diligence and to take all necessary precautions to ensure that they have formed a business relationship with reputable and qualified partners and representatives. Such due diligence may include investigating potential foreign representatives and joint venture partners to determine if they are in fact qualified for the position, whether they have personal or professional ties to the government, the number and reputation of their clientele, and their reputation with the U.S. Embassy or Consulate and with local bankers, clients, and other business associates.

In addition, in negotiating a business relationship, the U.S. firm should be aware of so-called red flags. Example warning signs are:

- Unusual payment patterns or financial arrangements.
- A history of corruption in the country.
- A refusal by the foreign joint venture partner or representative to provide a certification that it will not take any action in furtherance of an

unlawful offer, promise, or payment to a foreign public official and not take any act that would cause the U.S. firm to be in violation of the FCPA.
- Unusually high commissions.
- Lack of transparency in expenses and accounting records.
- An apparent lack of qualifications or resources on the part of the joint venture partner or representative to perform the services offered.
- Whether the joint venture partner or representative has been recommended by an official of the potential governmental customer.

You should seek the advice of counsel and consider utilizing the DOJ's Foreign Corrupt Practices Act Opinion Procedure for particular questions relating to third-party payments.

Facilitating Payments

The FCPA contains an explicit exception to the bribery prohibition for "facilitating payments" for "routine governmental action" and provides affirmative defenses that can be used to defend against alleged violations of the FCPA.

Facilitating Payments for Routine Governmental Actions

There is an exception to the anti-bribery prohibition for payments to facilitate or expedite performance of a "routine governmental action." The statute lists the following examples: obtaining permits, licenses, or other official documents; processing governmental papers, such as visas and work orders; providing police protection; providing mail pickup and delivery; providing phone service, power and water supply, loading and unloading cargo services, or protecting perishable products; and scheduling inspections associated with contract performance or transit of goods across country.

Actions "similar" to these are also covered by this exception. If you have a question about whether a payment falls within the exception, you should consult with counsel. You should also consider whether to utilize the DOJ's Foreign Corrupt Practices Opinion Procedure, described in the next section.

"Routine governmental action" does not include any decision by a foreign official to award new business or to continue business with a particular party.

Affirmative Defenses

A person charged with a violation of the FCPA's anti-bribery provisions may assert as a defense that the payment was lawful under the written laws of the foreign country or that the money was spent as part of demonstrating a product or performing a contractual obligation.

Whether a payment was lawful under the written laws of the foreign country may be difficult to determine. You should consider seeking the advice of counsel or utilizing the DOJ's Foreign Corrupt Practices Act Opinion Procedure when faced with an issue of the legality of such a payment.

Moreover, because these defenses are "affirmative defenses," the defendant is required to show in the first instance that the payment met these requirements. The prosecution does not bear the burden of demonstrating in the first instance that the payments did not constitute this type of payment.

Sanctions against Bribery

Criminal

The following criminal penalties may be imposed for violations of the FCPA's anti-bribery provisions: corporations and other business entities are subject to a fine of up to $2 million; officers, directors, stockholders, employees, and agents are subject to a fine of up to $100,000 and imprisonment for up to five years. Moreover, under the Alternative Fines Act, these fines may be actually quite higher—the actual fine may be up to twice the benefit that the defendant sought to obtain by making the corrupt payment. You should also be aware that fines imposed on individuals may not be paid by the defendant's employer or principal.

Civil

The attorney general or the SEC, as appropriate, may bring a civil action for a fine of up to $10,000 against any firm as well as any officer, director, employee, or agent of a firm, or stockholder acting on behalf of the firm, who violates the anti-bribery provisions. In addition, in an SEC enforcement action, the court may impose an additional fine not to exceed the greater of (1) the gross amount of the pecuniary gain to the defendant as a result of the violation, or (2) a specified dollar limitation. The specified dollar limitations are based on the egregiousness of the violation, ranging from $5,000 to $100,000 for a natural person and $50,000 to $500,000 for any other person.

The attorney general or the SEC, as appropriate, may also bring a civil action to enjoin any act or practice of a firm whenever it appears that the firm (or an officer, director, employee, agent, or stockholder acting on behalf of the firm) is in violation (or about to be) of the anti-bribery provisions.

Other Governmental Action

Under guidelines issued by the Office of Management and Budget, a person or firm found in violation of the FCPA may be barred from doing business with the federal government. Indictment alone can lead to suspension of the right to do business with the government. The president has directed that no executive agency shall allow any party to participate in any procurement or nonprocurement activity if any agency has debarred, suspended, or otherwise excluded that party from participation in a procurement or nonprocurement activity.

Additional aspects of the FCPA include:

- A person or firm found guilty of violating the FCPA may be ruled ineligible to receive export licenses.
- The SEC may suspend or bar persons from the securities business and impose civil penalties on persons in the securities business for violations of the FCPA.
- The Commodity Futures Trading Commission and the Overseas Private Investment Corporation both provide for possible suspension or debarment from agency programs for violation of the FCPA.
- A payment made to a foreign government official that is unlawful under the FCPA cannot be deducted under the tax laws as a business expense.

Conduct that violates the anti-bribery provisions of the FCPA may also give rise to a private cause of action for treble damages under the Racketeer Influenced and Corrupt Organizations Act (RICO), or to actions under other federal or state laws. For example, an action might be brought under RICO by a competitor who alleges that the bribery caused the defendant to win a foreign contract.

CHAPTER 6

Internal Controls and Accounting Provisions of the FCPA

William P. Olsen and Kelly Gentenaar

In the age of multinational, global corporations, compliance professionals cannot afford to simply be reactive when a potential Foreign Corrupt Practices Act (FCPA) violation occurs. They must be proactive advocates of a control environment that prevents FCPA violations.

During the past several years, the FCPA has enjoyed an unprecedented spotlight as the U.S. Securities and Exchange Commission (SEC) and the U.S. Department of Justice (DOJ) have increasingly turned to the act to penalize domestic and overseas companies, as well as individuals, suspected of bribing foreign officials to secure business. The DOJ and the SEC initiated 38 FCPA matters in 2007, as compared to only 6 in 2003. In 2008, FCPA matters initiated totaled 25. In the first six months of 2009, the SEC and DOJ initiated 19 enforcement actions. Additionally, fines and penalties related to FCPA matters have increased dramatically.

The Siemens AG settlement announced on December 15, 2008, was the largest settlement to date, at $1.6 billion. At the announcement of the Siemens settlement, Linda Chatman Thomsen, director of the Division of Enforcement of the SEC, noted that the SEC portion of the settlement ($350 million) was 10 times larger than the largest prior SEC FCPA settlement. As the number of investigations and settlements continues to grow, it is critical for companies, and specifically compliance professionals, to ensure the appropriate control environment is established, maintained, and monitored.

FCPA Accounting Provisions

When assessing controls, it is important to remember that the FCPA contains two separate aspects: anti-bribery and accounting provisions.

The accounting provisions require that companies maintain books, records, and accounts that accurately and fairly reflect, in reasonable detail, the transactions and dispositions of assets of the company. Companies are also required to devise and maintain a system of internal accounting controls that provide reasonable assurance that transactions are executed in accordance with management's general or specific authorization.

Transactions must be recorded to permit preparation of financial statements in conformity with generally accepted accounting principles or any other criteria applicable to such statements. Accountability of assets must be maintained. Access to assets must be permitted only in accordance with management's general and specific authorization. The recorded accountability for assets must be compared with the existing assets at reasonable intervals, and appropriate action must be taken with respect to differences.

Failed Controls

On May 29, 2009, the SEC settled an enforcement action against Thomas Wurzel, the former president of ACL Technologies, Inc. (ACL), and a related administrative proceeding against the former parent company of ACL, United Industrial Corporation (UIC). Both settlements were reached without the defendants admitting or denying the allegations.

The allegations against Mr. Wurzel stated that the former president authorized payments to an agent in order to secure contracts with the Egyptian Air Force (EAF). The administrative order against UIC stated, "... UIC lacked internal controls sufficient to detect or prevent improper payments such as those made by ACL to the EAF Agent." Specifically, Mr. Wurzel was able to authorize large payments to the EAF agent without meaningful substantiation or supporting documents.

Documentation provided by the EAF agent indicated that the payments were for "consulting" or "marketing services," without meaningful records detailing the services being provided. Furthermore, the initial payments (as early as 1997) were authorized to the EAF agent in the absence of a written contract with the EAF agent or documented due diligence having been conducted. Internal policies of UIC, instituted in 1999, required that any employee wishing to engage the services of a foreign agent submit due diligence forms prior to corporate counsel's granting approval. Due diligence forms for the EAF agent were not submitted until 2002. Additionally, although UIC's regulatory compliance policy required certain representations specific to FCPA compliance to be included in contracts, these representations were not included in the EAF Agent's contract until 2003.

As the UIC case illustrates, it is not enough to document internal controls through policies. In order to ensure compliance with the FCPA, the control environment must be cultivated through clearly articulated and monitored control activities that prevent management override. Furthermore, monitoring of internal controls needs to be vigilant and substantive to ensure that policies and procedures are followed in all cases. Compliance professionals should be aware that creating a documented anti-corruption program does not, in and of itself, create a control environment.

Controls Assessment

Controls must be assessed for both design and operating effectiveness. The accounting provisions of the FCPA do not specifically call for the development of FCPA-related control activities. The elegance of the act is that the books and records provisions implicitly promote an environment where violations of the anti-bribery provisions do not occur.

In conducting an FCPA controls assessment, one must identify and understand the risk factors systemic to the industry and unique to the company. Simply stated: (1) where are you doing business?, (2) who are you doing business with?, and (3) how are you doing business?

Where Are You Doing Business?

Conducting business in geographic locations where corruption risks are high necessitates a stronger level of control activity for those specific locations. Design of controls must take into account the risk profile of the countries where your company operates and known areas of corruption specific to your industry. Controls for countries or regions with high-risk profiles should include greater oversight of accounting and purchasing functions. Additionally, to determine if controls are operating effectively, monitoring of activities, through such means as internal audit, should be more frequent for higher-risk geographies.

Who Are You Doing Business With?

FCPA risks increase where your potential customers are government agencies or state-owned enterprises. If you do business with these types of customers, activities such as meals and entertainment or travel related to customer demonstrations must be evaluated for FCPA implications. Controls should be established to identify government-related customers. Furthermore, controls must be implemented to identify expenses related to these customers and ensure appropriate authorization.

How Are You Doing Business?

The use of consultants or marketing personnel as "agents" to help develop business significantly increases FCPA risk. Policies and procedures for retaining and contracting agents should be developed and implemented. Due diligence on the agents should be conducted to ensure a solid understanding of the type of individual or vendor engaged to represent the company. Furthermore, documentation of payments to agents (such as banking details) should be compiled during contracting and compared to payment instructions received with invoices from the agent to ensure that discrepancies do not exist.

Compliance professionals can be at the mercy of overseas operations for the identification of new vendors as agents. In order to ensure that all agents are identified prior to engagement, monitoring of general ledger accounts (such as consulting, marketing, and legal fees) should be conducted. Other types of transactions, such as charitable or political contributions, should require prior approval, and these general ledger accounts should be monitored. Additionally, controls should be implemented relating to regulatory relationships such as licenses, permits, and other approvals. In addition to established business operations, controls must be assessed for FCPA implications in business acquisitions, joint ventures, and business partnerships. Compliance professionals should be included in new business venture discussions to ensure that risks are appropriately mitigated before a new endeavor is undertaken.

Conclusion

Compliance with both anti-bribery and accounting provisions of the FCPA must be fostered through a strongly implemented control environment. Developing this environment is an enterprise-wide process that not only should include the compliance professionals of an organization, but also corporate officers, other management, the board of directors (particularly the audit committee), the finance department, and internal audit. The "tone from the top," communicated through corporate correspondence such as policies and procedures, actions of management, and training, is the foundation for the control environment.

Building from that foundation, control activities—designed appropriately and operating effectively—should be continually assessed to ensure that FCPA risks have been mitigated. Furthermore, as the company evolves with new business enterprises and the changing global economy, compliance professionals must provide input into the assessment of risks associated with new operations, whether related to new business or geography. Finally, control design, as well as control operating effectiveness, should be continually assessed in order to ensure that policy and procedural and, ultimately, regulatory compliance is obtained.

Having a robust anti-corruption program will not only assist an organization in detecting and deterring violations of the FCPA, but it will also help in mitigating fines and penalties if violations do occur. Being able to demonstrate that top management set the proper tone from the top and was proactive in monitoring for compliance with anti-corruption policies and procedures will be very helpful when dealing with regulators and prosecutors and when trying to separate the actions of individuals from those of the organization.

Finally, the financial impact of the loss in business reputation when a violation occurs can often be more severe than the fines and penalties for a violation. When all of this is taken into account, it is clear that there is a very strong business case for adopting a proactive approach to mitigating the risks of an FCPA violation.

Case Study: Rolling on a River

Business Challenge

A publicly traded U.S. company was hired to dredge a river in Southeast Asia by the local government. The company employed an agent who secured the work through his wife, who was related to a high-ranking government official. A whistle-blower alleged that the U.S. company representatives were bribing government officials. The chief financial officer felt that there was no possibility of fraud because the project was running at a 28% profit margin.

Investigation

The investigation concluded that the company officials engaged in a scheme to bribe government inspectors to approve invoices for work that was never completed. The agent acted as the liaison with the government officials receiving the bribes and received a "commission" for his services. The agent's wife acted as the bookkeeper for the project and admitted keeping two sets of books and falsifying reports to the local government. The agent had previously met with company auditors to discuss the details of the project; an e-mail was later uncovered, from the agent to the project manager, stating,

"He wined and dined the auditors and sent them back down the river." The investigation also uncovered evidence of bribes and kickbacks on other government projects.

Result

The investigation resulted in the resignation of the company's president and the rescinding of millions of dollars in fraudulent invoices. The government assigned a blue-ribbon panel of senators to investigate corruption on government contracts. The company paid heavy fines and penalties for False Claims and corruption violations.

Sample FCPA Work Plan

1. Evaluate comprehensiveness of Client's Policies and Procedures/Ethics Rules relating to FCPA compliance, including Delegations of Authority to approve or reject requests by Client personnel or agents to take actions covered by FCPA.
2. Work with company counsel on understanding key compliance program attributes at the local office level, such as:
   a. Use of FCPA language with contractors, suppliers, agents, etc.
   b. Having key employees sign an FCPA acknowledgment.
   c. Adequacy of FCPA training and related training/reference materials.
   d. Monitoring of employee certification process.
3. Discuss the overall adequacy of internal controls with representatives from local office and local accounting firm personnel. Obtain and discuss any significant management recommendations and evaluate their impact on the accounting control environment.
4. Review existing communicated standards from the Company to the local country Company personnel with respect to FCPA accounting and record-keeping requirements.
5. Perform preliminary interviews of key personnel to gain an understanding of overall operations and adequacy of record keeping. Obtain and review any existing key accounting policy statements or similar documentation that addresses basic accounting controls and processes. Evaluate the stated policy with respect to key areas designed to ensure the adequacy of books and records, such as:
   a. Vendor approval/contracting process (including specific process used with respect to consultants, agents, zoning/site facilitators, public relations firms, etc.)
   b. Vendor payment process
   c. "Petty" cash process

    d. Hiring and related payroll process, especially with respect to "temporary" labor

6. Review the accounts payable process to ensure that proper segregation of duties and authorization requirements are in place and being adhered to.

7. Review selected contracts to assure that proper FCPA clauses are included in all agreements.

8. Review selected employee folders to assure that employees are signing FCPA agreements and that their agreements are being maintained properly.

9. Discuss with applicable local office personnel the nature of any existing compliance function, including any internal audit group, inside legal counsel, etc. Consider impact of any existing resources and their actions on the extent and nature of further work.

10. Review general ledgers and supporting detailed accounting records, looking for unusual activity and/or suspicious vendors (i.e., large round numbers, multiple payments for same amount, etc.).

11. Review payments made to consultants and similar vendors, with particular attention paid to the purpose of the payment and the nature and extent of the service provided. Such review should include the review of large round dollar payments, offshore transfers, and unusually high expense amounts. This review should be focused on expenses for consulting, training, miscellaneous, temporary labor, commissions, loans, legal fees, travel, entertainment, and similar payments.

12. Review payments made to individuals, agents, and intermediaries, including distributors, dealers, directors, and joint venture partners (including employees), to determine the purpose of the payment. Review payroll and perform tests to ensure that all employees exist and are performing services.

13. Review supporting documentation for all cash advances, travel advances, commissions, bonuses, wire transfers, and other cash disbursements for selected senior management personnel and expatriates.

14. Review all significant petty cash activity for unusual or unsupported payments.

15. Review due diligence policies and procedures for vendors and consultants.

16. Depending on the results of other procedures performed, consider performing background checks on selected vendor agents and consultants to identify potential conflicts of interest or government association.

17. Review current Office of Foreign Assets Control (OFAC) and Department of Commerce listings of restricted and sanctioned entities and compare to Client's vendors.

18. Perform interviews of selected employees, vendors, agents, or consultants regarding specific transactions identified in order to obtain a better understanding of the nature and purpose of the transaction.
19. Review e-mail activity and computer files of selected employees, vendors, agents, and consultants.

CHAPTER 7

Do Not Crimp[1]

The Need for Oversight of Foreign Operations

William P. Olsen

With increased Securities and Exchange Commission (SEC) and Department of Justice (DOJ) scrutiny on U.S. companies, business practices in foreign countries need to stay focused on the Foreign Corrupt Practices Act (FCPA).

In the wake of the Sarbanes-Oxley Act of 2002 (SOX), companies have invested significant time and money to ensure compliance with U.S. laws and regulations. However, these laws and regulations are the Achilles' heel of many U.S. companies with foreign operations. A myopic focus on home office policies and procedures can detract from oversight of overseas operations. In particular, significant risks exist when companies neglect to monitor for violations of the FCPA.

While the FCPA has been in place since the 1970s, there has been a recent spike in investigations by both the U.S. Securities and Exchange Commission (SEC) and the Department of Justice (DOJ). This current trend is the result of companies moving more aggressively into emerging markets like India and China, where anti-bribery laws tend to be somewhat lax. Provisions of SOX itself are another reason why scrutiny of FCPA violations has increased. Not only is there overall concern with corporate governance, prompting regulators to increase their watchfulness, but an important SOX provision encourages companies to set up whistle-blower programs to facilitate the reporting of fraud and other illegal activity. Whistle-blower programs have been proven to increase the reporting of suspicious activity.

---

[1] Reprinted with permission from *Financial Executive* (Jan/Feb. 2007). © by Financial Executives International; 973.765.1000; www.financialexecutives.org.

Additionally, because FCPA violations such as bribes and money laundering are often associated with terrorism, the DOJ has stepped up its vigilance.

As we stated earlier, penalties for violating the FCPA can be harsh. Companies that pay off foreign officials are liable for up to $2 million, or twice the gross gain or loss derived from the bribe. Individuals can be fined up to $250,000, or twice the gross gain or loss derived, and can incur a prison sentence of up to five years. Companies found guilty of improper and misleading record keeping can pay up to $2.5 million in fines; the repercussions for individuals are even more severe—these include a maximum $1 million fine and up to 10 years in prison.

Pitfalls of Emerging Markets

Many companies fail to evaluate the risks before entering a new market. Often, poorly trained employees assume a "when-in-Rome" attitude, not realizing that the local way of doing business may be a direct violation of U.S. laws and regulations. It does not help that U.S. companies that abide by these laws and regulations tend to face an uneven playing field, sometimes losing out to competitors from countries that do not adhere to such practices. Even when other countries do have similar legislation, it is not necessarily enforced with the same vigor as in the United States.

Prior to beginning business in a new country, it is important to thoroughly research the business environment. As mentioned earlier, the global organization, Transparency International (www.transparency.org), compiles a "corruption index" every year to help companies understand the potential risks arising in certain countries.

When trying to penetrate a new market, businesses will often hire agents or consultants to assist with activities such as obtaining licenses. These individuals know the local business community and have access to the right government officials; when they offer legitimate assistance, they are a real asset. However, agents can pose risks because while some act properly, others do not. Often, relatives of foreign officials who have decision-making authority may set up consulting firms to facilitate transactions for foreign businesses. Paying individuals in such positions of influence can be considered a violation of the FCPA.

It is critical for companies to conduct a full background investigation of any agent or consultant they hire. Some federal agencies like the Department of Commerce and the Department of State will even assist with that process (they keep lists of individuals who have had previous FCPA violations). Such due diligence has an additional benefit: It creates a document trail that may be important if, despite its best efforts, a company is subject to an investigation. The company will then be able to show that it acted in good faith and tried to detect and deter FCPA violations.

Nevertheless, a background investigation is not always enough. Even after agents receive the green light, companies must continually monitor agent and employee activity. For example, if a company is paying an agent a flat fee for services and reimbursing expenses, the agent must show how that money is being used. Also, agents' contracts should clearly state that any violation of the FCPA is unacceptable—because, ultimately, the company can be held liable for that agent's actions.

The FCPA does acknowledge the complexities of conducting business in emerging markets. It includes exceptions that allow certain payments to help ease the transition into a country. These payments must be aimed at facilitating government procedures, as opposed to sidestepping them. For example, a company can hire an agency to facilitate the processing of employee passports and other paperwork. Similarly, many companies hire local representatives to help move equipment through customs quickly. This is normally considered legitimate, as long as the agency is not linked to government officials who oversee the process. The FCPA also allows companies to hire police protection to keep their employees safe.

Monitoring Behavior

To identify violations before the SEC does, companies should be aware of the following red flags:

- *Payments going offshore or to unusual addresses.* People involved in illegal activity want to put money in places where their government cannot get at it. For example, in Russia, payments may be going to the Cayman Islands. Both the Office of Foreign Assets Control (www.ustreas. gov/ofac) and the Financial Crimes Enforcement Network (www.fincen.gov) offer lists of known money laundering havens.
- *Frequent cash disbursements.* Distribution of large cash sums is often an indication that bribes are being doled out.
- *Overutilized accounts.* Accounts that cover payments for intangible services are often used to veil illegal payoffs. For example, if the legal accounts or consulting accounts appear overutilized, it is possible that illegal payoffs are being made. Companies should pay particular attention to activity in these accounts and demand supporting documentation for services rendered.
- *Lack of proper approval process.* Wire transfers typically require the sign-off of two high-ranking officials. However, employees involved in bribery or money laundering will often verbally approve wire transfers

because they do not want their signature on such transactions. Look for instances where managers have opted to override these internal controls.

- *Deals with complex legal structures.* When there are several layers of lawyers involved in a transaction, it is easy to lose track of payment flows. Funds that are ostensibly used to cover business meetings necessary for hashing out the details of a complex contract might instead be used for bribes. These types of expenditures should be examined closely, particularly when multiple firms are involved.

- *Unusually high or low profit margins on projects.* Profit margins cannot always be taken at face value. For example, profit margins might be high because no work is being performed. Very often, this red flag is ignored; so consider whether foreign operations are losing or making too much money.

- *Payments in round dollar amounts.* The Bank Secrecy Act requires financial institutions to report suspicious cash transactions. There is also a dollar threshold of $10,000, above which the filing of a Currency Transaction Report or a Suspicious Activity Report is required. Thus, companies involved in money laundering will often transfer funds in amounts just below the $10,000 reporting threshold, but often still in round numbers. If a company observes a series of transactions in round dollar amounts below the reporting threshold, this is a pattern that is consistent with money laundering activity and should be investigated.

Education and Communication

While it helps to know how to spot violations, knowing how to prevent them is even more important. The companies that are most successful in deterring FCPA violations usually do the following:

- *Educate employees about laws, regulations, and internal policies.* Employees being sent to manage foreign operations need to fully understand the provisions of the FCPA. Best-practice companies develop detailed training with interactive case material. They often require that employees sign an annual FCPA statement stating that they understand the act. This also documents that the company has been proactive in communicating that it will not tolerate improper business practices.

- *Provide mechanisms to report violations.* A comprehensive whistle-blower and complaint-handling process ensures that employees have a confidential means of notifying the home office of improper behavior.

- *Monitor for compliance.* Auditors, compliance officers, or ethics officers should have some formal involvement in overseeing foreign operations.

- *Respond quickly and appropriately to reported violations.* The worst thing an organization can do is to have suspicions raised and not properly respond to allegations. Not only is this a guaranteed way of running afoul of the regulators, it also sends a message down through the ranks that the company is not serious about punishing improper behavior.
- *At the first report of suspicious activity, the organization should conduct a prompt and thorough investigation.* It may need to disclose certain information to the SEC, terminate employees, or even walk away from a lucrative contract. Finally, the results of any investigation should be used to develop strategies for deterring future violations.

Extending the Tone from the Top beyond the Borders

The due diligence required to comply with the FCPA may mean that, in some cases, U.S. companies in emerging markets will not be as competitive as businesses from other nations. If a government investigation does occur, a strong FCPA program will reduce the risk of criminal prosecution or civil sanctions because regulators will consider whether the business fostered an anti-bribery culture or one where violations could thrive.

In the United States, SOX has placed companies on notice that intentional misrepresentation of their financial statements will not be tolerated. Thus, companies must remember that the importance of ethical and legal behavior does not stop when a company extends its operations overseas.

There is a common misperception that when "no one is watching," U.S. law does not apply. As the FCPA demonstrates, nothing could be further from the truth. Companies that believe otherwise do so at their own peril.

Case Study: Bribes in the USSR

Business Challenge

A privately held U.S. company acquired several Russian telecommunication companies and then planned to take the new global company public. The initial public offering (IPO) due diligence uncovered evidence of FCPA violations. The board of directors of the U.S. parent requested a full investigation.

Investigation

The investigation uncovered that one of the Russian entities employed an individual whose title was "Expert on Government Relations." His job, as he described it, was to "pay bribes to government officials." The controller of the company kept a ledger titled "Bribes to Government Officials," and many payments were made in cash from an account referred to as "Black Cash."

The investigation also uncovered that Russian government officials were on the payroll as temporary employees. Others were appointed to the company's board as directors and received director fee payments to an offshore bank account. The offshore account was listed on the FinCen watch list for known money laundering activity.

Results

The company self-reported to the DOJ and SEC. They were sanctioned with heavy fines and penalties and required to implement an ongoing compliance-monitoring program to assure the government that better controls had been implemented and no further violations had occurred. The company eventually went bankrupt under the weight of a second government investigation into more FCPA violations.

CHAPTER 8

The Human Factor[1]

Sri Ramamoorti and William P. Olsen

Eighty percent of respondents to a National Association of Corporate Directors (NACD) survey of public company audit committees felt that failure resulting from poor risk management could not happen to them. However, 50 percent thought it could happen to other companies.

This feeling of relative "invincibility" is similar to the statistically impossible "Lake Wobegon" effect—where "all the women are strong, all the men are good looking, and all the children are above average." Could this Lake Wobegon effect—which results from the human tendency to overestimate one's achievements and capabilities in relation to others—extend to an organization's assessment of its vulnerability to fraud risk?

Fraud is a human endeavor, involving deception, purposeful intent, intensity of desire, risk of apprehension, violation of trust, rationalization, and so on. So it is important to understand the psychological factors that might influence the behavior of fraud perpetrators. The rationale for drawing on behavioral science insights is evident from the intuition that one needs to "think like a crook to catch a crook."

Many business professionals, especially those in the finance arena, tend to discount behavioral explanations. But as the incidence of fraud continues to grow, placing the spotlight on behavioral factors may be an important approach to not only fraud detection, but to deterrence as well.

The 2006 *Report to the Nation* issued by the Association of Certified Fraud Examiners (ACFE) noted that U.S. organizations lose almost 5 percent of their revenue to fraud, and that the gross domestic product (GDP)-based annual fraud estimate for the United States was a whopping $652 billion. In

---

[1]Reprinted with permission from *Financial Executive* (July/Aug 2007). © by Financial Executives International; 973.765.1000; www.financialexecutives.org.

light of such sobering statistics, it behooves each and every organization to understand the root causes of fraud and proactively manage fraud risk.

Why Focus on Fraud and Corruption Risk?

Among the catastrophic risks afflicting organizations of all sizes is the risk of financial fraud. A single allegation of material fraud has such devastating financial consequences, including irreparable reputational damage, that few companies survive such a crisis unscathed. Fraud tends to be frequently a hidden risk, particularly because its perpetrators take extreme care to conceal their activities; hence, it also remains an unmanaged risk in organizations.

Nevertheless, it is rare that any company deliberately sets out to perpetrate a massive fraud. Instead, fraud is the unfortunate consequence of a multitude of mostly behavioral factors that drives otherwise honest people to do dishonest things. The sociology and criminology literature describes fraud perpetrators as "trust violators." In other words, trust violators are people you would not normally suspect of committing fraud.

Behavioral Root Causes of Fraud and Corruption

Much has been written about the root causes of fraud and the "fraud triangle," with its three vertices of opportunity, pressure/incentive and rationalization, as referred to in the ACFE 2005 *Fraud Examiner's Manual.*

What often goes unrecognized is that all three elements of the fraud triangle are fundamentally behavioral constructs. Personal incentives and perceived pressure drive human behavior, and the need to rationalize wrongdoing as being somehow defensible is very much psychologically rooted.

To some extent, even the assessment of the opportunity to commit fraud—including the likelihood of being caught—is a subjective, behavioral assessment. Accordingly, to understand the root causes of fraud, psychological answers and explanations rather than logical ones should be sought.

The decision to deviate from the norm and commit fraud is not taken lightly; it involves "rationalization," or the ability to justify one's own questionable actions to oneself and others. A tragic example is Enron Corporation's Cliff Baxter, who could not come to terms psychologically with what had happened and took the extraordinary step of committing suicide.

While corporate governance reform legislation such as the Sarbanes-Oxley Act of 2002 can help limit the opportunity for fraud, succumbing to perceived pressure and the ability to rationalize fraudulent acts are outside the scope of law. As such, fraud deterrence and detection should focus on how to deal with the underlying behavioral dynamics—the psychology of fraud perpetrators, as well as the psychology of those responsible for governance, including auditors.

Psychology of Fraud Perpetrators

An understanding of what motivates the fraudster, whether acting alone or in collusion with others within or outside an organization, can go a long way in identifying behavioral risk factors that may indicate fraud. A simple means/motive/opportunity analysis would show that motives are the crux of the matter, because fraud requires the establishment of intent to deceive another.

So it is crucial to know what it is that a fraud perpetrator desires: money (bonus, stock-based compensation), status ("keeping up with the Joneses," fame or celebrity status), revenge, a catch-me-if-you-can game, parity with others (everybody else is doing it, why can't I?), and so on.

If opportunities do not exist, the motivated fraud perpetrator can create them by a careful analysis of weaknesses in controls or by exploiting a generally lax environment. However, once fraud perpetrators take the initial steps, they frequently find themselves unable to turn back and escape the ruinous consequences.

Organizations must communicate to employees acceptable standards of behavior through a well-crafted code of conduct that is endorsed by leadership and enforced when necessary. Organizations should also develop a track record of acting swiftly and decisively whenever wrongdoing comes to light.

And, in every case, organizations must go to extreme lengths to protect a whistle-blower's identity and safety (from retaliation). Otherwise, potential fraud perpetrators are likely to exploit the inertia or complacency in addressing fraud risk adequately. As ACFE founder Joe Wells counsels, "Let them know you're watching."

Understanding Management Fraud

Thus, erstwhile honest and well-meaning executives who have earned the trust of others are often the ones who end up perpetrating fraud. Fraud does not start with dishonesty; it starts with pressure: Pressure to achieve aggressive financial performance goals, or meet analyst expectations, frequently leads those who are expected to make the numbers to simply "make up" the numbers. Like many other organizational risks, fraud usually starts small before it snowballs and becomes widespread, rampant, and material. Not surprisingly, the gray areas of accounting ripe for abuse are those that are complex, ambiguous, and subjective. Complexity can help mask fraud.

Among reasons managers cook the books are to:

- Meet analyst expectations and forecasts about earnings.
- Smooth earnings and income to reduce volatility (to mask financial distress and negative cash flows).
- Benefit from compensation or bonuses tied to earnings or to stay within debt covenants imposed by lenders.
- Avoid sanctions by deliberately deflating current earnings or to win subsidies or import relief as a protectionist advantage.
- Cover up bribes and kickbacks used to influence government officials.

In such contexts, the award of executive stock options provides further incentives to manipulate earnings, including enlisting the support and cooperation of junior, economically dependent, and vulnerable staff and employees.

In all circumstances, tone from the top is critical, and there is no excuse for senior executives or other employees to be active participants in a corrupt organizational culture.

Approaches to Deterring and Mitigating Financial Fraud Risk

From an organizational perspective, the goal is to create an environment that endorses a "good ethics is good business" philosophy, encourages doing the right thing at every turn, and makes perpetrating fraud an unattractive option to most people in the organization.

It is true that economics and ethics do not mix very well—there are numerous examples of how incentives have trumped personal ethics and values. Nevertheless, cultural assimilation into a system of high integrity and values represents a form of programming of the human mind that cannot be easily compromised. A culture of ethics has significant potential in reducing integrity risks. Rewarding people for doing the right thing sends the right signal to others in the organization, while shooting the messenger, in the case of a whistle-blower allegation, sends the wrong signal.

To discharge their monitoring and oversight function effectively, audit committees need a primer on the psychology of the fraud perpetrator(s), as well as insight about their own and the auditors' cognitive weaknesses.

The audit committee, with assistance from the internal and external auditors, as well as other risk management specialists and the board, is responsible for monitoring the behavior of management, especially with respect to financial reporting. However, in the current corporate governance climate, this mandate sometimes extends beyond financial reporting matters.

One important behavioral insight is recognizing that high-level fraud and corruption is frequently a team sport that often involves collusion. Internal control systems that presume proper segregation of duties are not effective against collusion and management override of controls. In fact, a Committee of Sponsoring Organizations of the Treadway Commission (COSO) Fraud Study published in 1999 found that in 83 percent of the frauds examined, the chief executive officer (CEO) and the chief financial officer (CFO) had colluded.

Still another problematic area is the well-known "groupthink" bias at the board level. Groupthink discounts contrarian opinions or tends to sway the group into making a "feel-good" decision. When there is an active tendency to ignore bad news due to either indifference or sheer laziness, board members may miss important signals of potential fraud.

External and internal auditors need to learn that "absence of evidence is not evidence of absence." The fact that no red flags or fraud indicia are observed does not mean that fraud does not exist. The trusted relationships that subsist between external auditors and their clients sometimes make auditors let their guard down.

When encountering fraud scenarios, human tendencies such as the confirmation bias (seeking confirmation of one's beliefs) and selective perception (seeing only what one wants to see) limit auditors' ability to exercise an appropriate level of professional skepticism.

Interestingly, the significance of behavioral science insights increases even more when we move into the domain of the global marketplace. This environment only creates more risks for U.S. organizations if their employees are not properly trained and prepared for risk of corruption. All too often, employees take a "when in Rome" attitude toward their business practices, not realizing that they are still answerable to U.S. laws and regulations. The end result can be catastrophic for the individuals as well as the organization.

CHAPTER 9

Corporate Governance

The Key to Unmasking Corrupt Activity

William P. Olsen

S ometimes the media has been overrun with stories of corporate fraud. As these reports depict, allegations and incidents of fraud have the potential to severely blemish—and possibly destroy—an organization's reputation among staff, vendors, and customers.

Because of the high level of trust that is the core of an organization's reputation, public relations issues are probably the largest and most unforeseen risks that come out of any type of fraudulent activity. While the immediate focus is often directed at cash loss, that is not always the greatest damage done. The organization's reputation suffers, which can translate into larger customer and financial losses long term. The potential financial and reputation loss associated with fraud has given rise to the need for solid corporate governance procedures.

Enterprise Risk Management: Create Stronger Governance and Corporate Compliance

More frequently than not, shareholders and regulators are now demanding greater corporate transparency, making strong corporate governance a necessary component to almost every business. Enterprise risk management (ERM) can contribute to successful, compliant, and effective governance, enabling companies to better understand and measure those risks that threaten strategic objectives. Moreover, ERM provides information that helps quantify business performance, narrow the focus of controls, and streamline compliance efforts.

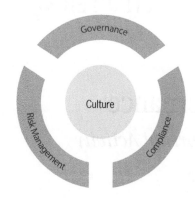

Governance
- Set and evaluate performance against objectives
- Empower to authorize a business strategy and model to achieve objectives

Risk Management
- Proactively identify and rigorously assess and address potential obstacles to achieving objectives
- Identify and address risks that the organization will step outside of mandated and voluntary boundaries

Culture
- Establish an organizational climate and mind-sets of individuals that promote ethical behavior, trust, integrity, and accountability

Compliance
- Proactively encourage and require compliance with established policies
- Detect noncompliance and respond accordingly

FIGURE 9.1 Integrated Governance, Risk, and Compliance (GRC)

As part of this process, some organizations have begun to use their risk objectives to create an integrated governance, risk, and compliance (GRC) management framework to help drive their compliance initiatives (Figure 9.1). This strategy is promoted by the Open Compliance and Ethics Group (OCEG). By establishing a GRC framework, companies are able to set their governance and enterprise risk objectives first, and then use these objectives to define compliance control requirements.

Governance

- Set and evaluate performance against objectives.
- Empower to authorize a business strategy and model to achieve objectives.

Culture

- Establish an organizational climate and mind-sets of individuals that promote ethical behavior, trust, integrity, and accountability.

Risk Management

- Proactively identify and rigorously assess and address potential obstacles to achieving objectives.

- Identify and address risks that the organization will step outside of mandated and voluntary boundaries.

Compliance

- Proactively encourage and require compliance with established policies.
- Detect noncompliance and respond accordingly.

Furthermore, the integration of governance, risk management, culture, and compliance can also help an organization more effectively and efficiently drive performance. Governance establishes objectives and, at a high level, the boundaries an entity must operate within. Risk management helps a company identify and address potential obstacles to achieving objectives. Compliance management ensures that the boundaries are well set, and that the organization does indeed conduct business within those boundaries. Finally, a strong culture provides a safety net when formal controls and structures are weak or nonexistent, while at the same time providing an environment that helps the workforce reach its highest level of productivity. High-performing organizations master and integrate these disciplines for maximum effectiveness and responsiveness, allowing their companies to leverage innovation in one area across the entire enterprise to address all set requirements.

Last, but certainly not least, an effective ERM program enhances a company's governance structure in that the "tone at the top" message is promulgated as one where compliance with laws, regulations, and internal policies and procedures is mandatory, and noncompliance is unacceptable. This assists in motivating desired conduct and provides assurance to management that they are operating within legal, contractual, internal, social, and ethical boundaries. Moreover, ERM further assists in establishing the fundamentals of a good governance environment and structure, promoting a common risk language and collaboration on risk management issues throughout the organization (e.g., sharing of any risk issues identified by internal audit, compliance officer, and others).

Mitigating Risk

The responsibility of mitigating the risk of fraud within an organization, or any business, falls on the shoulders of management and the board of directors.

Establishing effective corporate governance policies and procedures should be a top priority for any business today and indicates that the tone from the top sets the pace for how an organization and its employees conduct business.

Management is the standard-setting example for the corporate value system and should be proactive in policing and enforcing an established code of conduct. A code of conduct should be created with the input of management and the board and reviewed annually. A reliable and realistic code of ethics includes policies that are earnestly promoted and actively communicated by management.

In addition to a code of ethics, management and the board should assess the effectiveness of its internal controls and test them annually. An established, tested set of internal controls can help organizations ensure that they are in compliance with legislation and government regulations, and mitigate the risk of unexpected losses or mistakes that could damage the organization's reputation.

Ascertain Risk Areas

The board of directors should be active in the risk assessment process, thoroughly understanding the company's key business and financial reporting risks and the control processes and procedures established to manage those risks. Some risks to consider are:

- *Geographic risk*. Where are we doing business? What is the risk of corruption in that location?
- *Industry risk*. What risks are inherent to our industry? Is corruption one of them?
- *Technology risk*. How secure are our computer systems?
- *Organizational risk*. Does management set the right tone from the top?
- *Regulatory risk*. What laws and regulations apply to our business, and are we in compliance?
- *Reputation risk*. What types of events would cause the most damage to our organization's business reputation?

The board should:

- Assess the timeliness and substance of management's response to recommendations made by the organization's internal audit function and independent auditor.
- Understand and assess management's and the auditors' views on controlling financial reporting risks.
- Inquire about the root causes of significant financial adjustments.
- Respond appropriately to any allegation or suspicions of any illegal or unethical activity.

The new Federal Acquisition Regulation (FAR) Requirements for Contractor Compliance and Integrity Programs is a good example of proactive governance program. The new regulations add three new ethics requirements:

1. *Contractor Code of Business Ethics.* This requires implementing a written code of business ethics and conduct and providing a copy of the code to each employee engaged in performance of the contract.
2. *Business Conduct Awareness Program and Internal Control System.* These require implementing an ongoing business ethics and business conduct awareness program and implementing an internal control system that will facilitate timely discovery of improper conduct in connection with government contracts and ensure that corrective measures are promptly instituted and carried out.
3. *Communication of Fraud Hotline.* During contract performance in the United States, the contractor shall prominently display in common work areas within business segments performing work under this contract, and at contract work sites: (1) any agency fraud hotline poster or Department of Homeland Security fraud hotline poster, and (2) if the contractor maintains a company web site as a means of providing information to employees, the contractor shall display an electronic version of the posters on the web site.

The lack of an anti-corruption program should raise a red flag with auditors and can be a real weakness in a company's internal controls. Without a mechanism in place where employees can report suspicions or allegations, the illegal and unethical activity may never be reported. Establishing a code of ethics, effective internal controls, and an anti-corruption program are just several of the steps organizations should consider when putting together a corporate governance program. Developing corporate governance policies is an ongoing, evolving process.

Establishing Procedures to Mitigate Risk

To effectively mitigate risk, organizations need to identify procedures that control risk and identify weaknesses within the internal control system. Management should:

- Establish reporting and control objectives, assign control responsibilities, and train employees on operating and evaluating controls.
- Map business processes, document the flow of information, and identify all relevant control objectives and risks.

- Determine a corrective action plan and timetables for implementation where control weaknesses are noted. Disclose weaknesses and corrective actions to the board and the company's independent auditor.

Perform a Periodic Assessment

Organizations should establish an internal audit function, either developed in-house or outsourced, to annually rate internal control effectiveness. An internal audit function can evaluate the design and test the operating effectiveness of key controls.

Corporate governance policies should also encompass internal control processes that address how suspected illegal and unethical activities are reported and subsequently handled.

Blowing the Whistle on Corporate Fraud

Internal corporate corruption is often brought to the attention of management by company employees, or whistle-blowers. Companies do not always have policies in place through which employees who suspect illegal or unethical activity can voice their concerns confidentially and anonymously.

Setting up a whistle-blowing procedure is not a luxury in today's business environment—it is a requirement. To protect themselves, companies must put procedures in place for reporting fraudulent activity.

Hotlines are used by many companies, while other companies use an internal resource such as a chief compliance officer, human resources officer, or internal audit director, who is charged with investigating any allegations or suspicions of illegal or unethical activity.

Most importantly, employees should feel comfortable that they can remain anonymous if they choose to, and that there is going to be a prompt and skilled investigation in response to the allegations. If they do not think that is going to happen, chances are they will not report suspicious activity.

CHAPTER 10

Whistle-Blower Programs

Brad Preber and Trent Gazzaway

In 2002, the Sarbanes-Oxley Act (SOX) breathed new life into whistle-blower programs for U.S.-listed public companies. This legislation had a particular impact on audit committees, handing them the responsibility of "establishing procedures for (a) the receipt, retention, and treatment of complaints received by the issuer regarding accounting, internal accounting controls, or auditing matters; and (b) the confidential, anonymous submission by employees of the issuer of concerns regarding questionable accounting or auditing matters."

SOX, however, did not provide any guidance to audit committees on what procedures should be considered or how to evaluate their effectiveness once established. As a result, for many companies, complaint handling is still a haphazard process that tends to operate in crisis mode. It can be both costly and time consuming, yielding few, if any, measurable results. We have found that, even now, almost four years after the enactment of SOX, companies are still struggling to find an effective approach to handling whistle-blower complaints.

It is important to understand the role whistle-blower complaint handling plays in deterring corporate fraud. Controls on the front end that prevent or deter fraud are critical—after all, the cheapest fraud is one that never happens. An effective whistle-blower program, however, is the last line of defense.

According to the Association of Certified Fraud Examiners' (ACFE's) 2008 Report to the Nation, a study of 959 cases of occupational fraud, the most expensive forms of fraud are not detected as a result of internal controls. This is in part because perpetrators of fraud work in areas that are not tightly controlled or in areas that they themselves control. By far, the most effective form of fraud detection is a tip, often received via a fraud hotline.

However, in the ACFE study, whistle-blower hotlines, which also detected the largest fraud losses, were one of the least common anti-fraud mechanisms in use.

For the most part, what has been lacking both from the literature and from practice is a methodical approach that organizations can use to register complaints and channel them to the appropriate groups for action. Only by establishing a comprehensive process will organizations be able to ensure that, when the whistle does blow, someone has the wherewithal to stop the train, get out, and investigate.

Pulling Out the Earplugs

In recent years, there have been numerous examples of companies that have taken a "hear no evil" approach to whistle-blower complaints. The SOX requirements regarding whistle-blower programs are an indication that organizations must have processes in place that guarantee these complaints are heard and dealt with appropriately.

Procedures must "facilitate disclosures, encourage proper individual conduct, and alert the audit committee to potential problems before they have serious consequences." Table 10.1 more fully describes these requirements.

TABLE 10.1 Whistleblower Complaint-Handling Requirements

Requirement	Definition
Facilitate disclosures	Discover, in a timely manner, evidence of activities that may threaten or impede compliance with laws, rules, regulations, and standards related to financial statements and associated disclosures, regulatory filings, and other public disclosures.
Encourage proper individual conduct	Provide a process that, when implemented and properly maintained, will assist in efforts to reinforce predefined and acceptable ethical behaviors related to accounting, internal accounting controls, or auditing matters or, alternatively, will prevent, or detect and correct, unacceptable conduct.
Alert the audit committee, or other governing body, to potential problems before they have serious consequences	Establish an "early warning system" to bring accounting, internal accounting control, and auditing matters to the attention of the audit committee in time to prevent, or detect and correct, possible problems before they cause serious harm or damage.

In response to this challenge, we have developed a process called the Model Accounting Complaint-Handling Process, or "MACH Process," for dealing with whistle-blower complaints swiftly and efficiently in connection with accounting, internal controls over financial reporting, and auditing matters. As the term *MACH* implies, this process is intended to effectively deal with complaints as quickly as possible.

The MACH Process is designed to provide both meaningful structure and enough flexibility so that it can be adapted to any organization. It should not be viewed as a soup-to-nuts formula for setting up a whistle-blower program. Instead, the MACH Process focuses on the component of any whistle-blower program that requires the most attention from management and the board—handling complaints once they are received. Setting up the overall program is important, including making decisions regarding whether to insource or outsource the program administration, who to engage, how to handle different countries' related legal requirements, and so on. The focus here is on what happens once the whistle blows and that train starts rolling down the track.

Understanding Stakeholders and Their Needs

A critical first step to customizing the MACH Process is identifying stakeholders and understanding their disparate needs. There are three primary sets of stakeholders in the MACH Process:

1. *Users:* Individuals who file whistle-blower complaints.
2. *The accused:* Individuals, groups (e.g., departments) or companies that are the focus of the complaint.
3. *Other interested parties:* Stakeholders with a vested interest in the asserted claim, investigation, and/or outcome.

Users, the accused, and others can be either inside or outside the company. A key for the successful use of the MACH Process is to identify all potential stakeholders of the system.

Whistle-blower complaints are typically received from internal sources like employees (sometimes former employees), management, and directors. Likewise, those implicated by whistle-blower complaints are usually insiders. Complaints received from outside the company may be from customers, vendors, suppliers, or investors. Conversely, parties external to the company are often suspects in purchase schemes, bribery, and overbilling scams.

A complaint and the related investigation impact a wider circle than just the whistle-blower and the suspect. A range of other interested parties is either directly involved in the investigation or requires information at different phases of the process.

TABLE 10.2 Stakeholders in the Whistle-Blower Complaint-Handling Process

Stakeholder	Internal	External
Users (whistle-blowers)	Employees Management Directors/Officers	Customers Vendors Suppliers Investors
Accused parties	Employees Management Directors/Officers	Customers Vendors Suppliers Brokers
Other interested parties	General legal counsel Internal audit Risk management Information technology Human resources Public and investor relations	Outside legal counsel Bankers Insurance companies Government/regulators Rating agencies Shareholders External auditors Creditors Debtors

A list of potential stakeholders is summarized in Table 10.2. All of these stakeholders have different needs, which are rarely aligned. Acknowledging these many needs and tailoring the MACH Process to meet them are critical. It is up to the audit committee to identify, sufficiently understand, and consider the needs of each and every stakeholder in designing the MACH Process.

Internal Users

Anyone wishing to express a concern, especially if it involves accounting, controls, or auditing matters, should feel comfortable using the MACH Process and should be encouraged to do so. This is especially critical for internal users, who may have real apprehensions about whether filing a complaint will cost them their job or cause some other negative consequence.

Internally generated whistle-blower claims—asserted by directors, management, and employees—may be submitted in writing or provided orally. In general, internal sources will want the following from their company's MACH Process:

- *Choice of reporting venues.* Complaints may come from discussions with supervisors, confidential conversations with human resources personnel, anonymous "tip" lines, company web sites, and e-mail. Any of these venues needs to feed seamlessly into the MACH Process.

- *Confidentiality and anonymity.* SOX requires that the audit committees of public companies establish procedures for "the confidential, anonymous submission by employees of the issuer of concerns regarding questionable accounting controls or auditing matters." This creates the need for a process that accepts confidential complaints from anonymous sources with a high degree of assurance that confidentiality will be preserved. Otherwise, the motivation to be a whistle-blower will diminish significantly.
- *Ease of use.* Users of the MACH Process want to be able to pick up a phone or send an e-mail to make a complaint. They do not want to have to wade through layers of bureaucracy to make their concerns known. Furthermore, if it is not obvious to employees how to file a complaint, they are far less likely to come forward. A communications plan that encourages and facilitates use of the system will go a long way toward ensuring its use.
- *Information on progress of complaint.* This is an area that can be especially sensitive. Whistle-blowers want to know that their claims are being handled in an expeditious fashion and that the organization is working to resolve the issue; yet for highly sensitive complaints, it is important to protect the privacy of others impacted by the complaint and the organization itself. In such cases, progress reports may not be appropriate. The audit committee will have to consider such issues and develop policy guidelines in advance.

The whistle-blower complaint-handling process will not be fully adopted by potential users and stakeholders if they perceive that there are barriers to using the process or if it fails to effectively meet their needs. Therefore, potential obstacles should be identified and removed. A busy phone tip line, a breach of confidentiality, and an unanswered e-mail complaint are problems that cannot be ignored, or the process may fail.

To demonstrate the credibility and objectivity of the program to internal users, it is important to emphasize that the audit committee has sole responsibility for the receipt, handling, and investigation of accounting, internal control, and auditing matters. Tell employees that legal counsel will be used to protect them and the organization. Users will also gain confidence in the process if they are aware that investigations will include consultation with qualified advisers, both internal and external to the company.

External Users

External users are whistle-blowers outside the organization, such as vendors, customers, and suppliers. While it is not mandatory for claims from external sources to be kept anonymous, external sources have the same need as insiders for ready access to an appropriate venue to lodge complaints. This means that the audit committee should have established policies to receive such complaints and that company representatives must be trained and knowledgeable about the procedures to accept, report, and process an outsider's complaint.

The Accused

Parties who become targets of whistle-blower claims also need to be considered. Confidentiality is especially important because an individual accused of wrongdoing must be afforded due process and protection from unmerited personal and professional harm. Unless such situations are handled very carefully, individuals who have been wrongly accused can experience serious damage to their reputations, possibly jeopardizing their livelihoods. The audit committee therefore needs to develop a set of policies for handling the special needs of the accused. For example, one of the first questions arising when a whistle-blower investigation is undertaken is whether the suspect should be placed on administrative leave. This is an issue that normally requires the assistance of human resource professionals and legal counsel.

Other Interested Parties

On the other side of the table from the accused are stakeholders who will be impacted by the investigation. Their needs are generally quite simple: They want as much information as possible. Inside the company, management, employees, the audit committee, and other directors will have a need for information. In most cases, general counsel, internal audit personnel, risk management professionals, information technologists, and human resource personnel will be asked to assist the audit committee by gathering intelligence through research and interviews.

Investor, marketing, and public relations specialists, who will have responsibility for properly informing company personnel and the public about the matter, also have a stake.

Outside the company, others will be at risk and have a pressing need for information and access to insiders. This is why many companies struggle with disclosure issues after whistleblower complaints have been filed.

Shareholders want to be assured that their investment is safe, bankers may want to reassess lending risk, insurers will want to determine if the claim is covered, and rating agencies must measure the effect on creditworthiness. The external auditor will want to know if the company has assessed the impact on the financial statements. Also, anxious regulators and class-action lawyers will be quick to respond. To complicate matters, as the complaint moves through the system, the nature of these stakeholders may change.

Because the information needs of many interested parties may be in direct conflict with the confidentiality needs of the accused, the audit committee faces a balancing act in determining how much information to release and how much to withhold.

Audit committees should consider adopting a set of guidelines governing the distribution of information to different stakeholders to address their expected needs. For example, independent auditors should be notified when a significant financial statement complaint has been filed, or banks should be contacted if company cash accounts have been adversely impacted. Some complaints involve senior officers of the company who are covered by indemnification agreements. In these cases, the guideline may be to inform legal counsel in order to have them analyze the agreements and determine whether the company is required to pay for the defense of the accused officer.

Possible governance considerations include:

- Has the company identified all potential stakeholders (users, the accused, and others) in the whistle-blowing process?
- Has the whistle-blowing process been extended to include outsiders such as customers and vendors?
- Are the needs of stakeholders in the whistle-blowing process sufficiently understood by the company?
- Has the whistle-blowing process been customized to meet key stakeholder needs?
- Has the company provided its employees with systems that are flexible, confidential, anonymous, and easy to use for filing a whistle-blower complaint?
- Has the company minimized obstacles to usage of the whistle-blower complaint-handling process?
- Does the audit committee have guidelines for addressing competing stakeholder needs for information once a complaint has occurred?

Steps of the MACH Process

The MACH Process (see Figure 10.1) consists of six basic steps:

1. Receive the complaint.
2. Analyze the complaint.
3. Investigate the complaint.

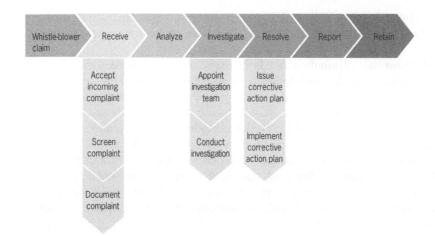

FIGURE 10.1 Steps of the Model Accounting Complaint-Handling (MACH) Process

4. Resolve the complaint.
5. Report the resolution of the complaint.
6. Retain the necessary documentation.

Step 1: Receive

The act of receiving a complaint might appear simple and intuitive but, in fact, it requires considerable planning to ensure that it is structured appropriately. Specifically, it needs to address:

- The method for documenting and housing claims, including appropriate training for those responsible for claim intake.
- The process for screening claims and determining if they need to be passed on to the audit committee.

ACCEPTING INCOMING COMPLAINTS   Each whistle-blower claim, whether oral or written, should be logged in and assigned a unique claim number for tracking and control purposes. This can also be an effective tool for preserving anonymity. A claims log is used to capture basic information in a standard format as soon as it is received. It also serves as a control at the end of the process to ensure all reported claims are handled. A claims log will include the following information:

- Claim number
- Date of claim

- Basic claim information, such as:
  - Source of complaint (i.e., internal, such as an employee, vs. external, such as a customer)
  - Suspected party, group, or company
- Outside source contact information (*Note:* internal sources must be kept confidential and anonymous at this point)
- Action based on recommendation from claims screening committee (see next section):
  - Dismissed (as irrelevant or unmerited)
  - Referred to the audit committee
  - Referred to another responsible party (such as human resources for a personnel issue or customer service for a client service matter)

If the whistle-blower submitting the claim is an employee, the interviewer should determine whether he or she desires anonymity, which is guaranteed under Section 301 of SOX. Waiving anonymity can sometimes speed up the investigation process by allowing the investigation team direct access to the whistle-blower. Often, the individual can also provide evidence in the form of documents and files, saving the team both time and effort.

SCREENING COMPLAINTS   Any claim that has the potential to materially impact the financial statements is the responsibility of the audit committee, yet if the audit committee were to review every whistle-blower claim, they would quickly be overwhelmed. For this reason, the MACH Process includes a screening step for each claim, which is the responsibility of a claims screening committee. Members of this group are appointed and overseen by the audit committee and may include:

- Audit committee member or appropriate designee
- Legal counsel (either internal or external)
- Internal audit (IA)
- Human resources (HR)
- Internal risk management

Alternatively, the duties of the claims screening committee may be delegated by the audit committee to an adequately trained and qualified outside service provider or consultant.

One of the biggest challenges in screening complaints is determining whether to pursue a specific matter based on the available facts. Frivolous complaints may be common, and disgruntled employees may simply want a vehicle for venting their frustrations. Moreover, complaints may not be indicative of fraudulent activity, or may be unrelated to accounting and auditing matters. Hence, a primary purpose of the claims screening committee is to examine each whistle-blower claim and determine whether it has:

- Merit (i.e., it is credible, valid, and not frivolous or unsubstantiated), in which case it will be referred to the appropriate governing body for further analysis and investigation. Any claim that has merit must be referred for investigation.
- Relevance to accounting, internal accounting controls, or auditing matters, in which case it will be referred to the audit committee for further analysis and investigation.

Many whistle-blower complaints reported through anonymous hotlines are likely to be HR-related and probably have no bearing on financial reporting. Nevertheless, many claims that, on their surface, would not be considered material to the financial statements may, in fact, have a very serious impact. For example, if a company receives complaints about age discrimination, this is not a financial statement issue per se. If it appears, however, that there is the potential for a class-action lawsuit, suddenly the picture is quite different. It is therefore important for the claims screening committee to think broadly about what is meant by "relevant to accounting, internal accounting controls, or auditing matters"; they need to continually ask, "What would the marketplace think?" because that is the real arbiter of financial statement impact.

The claims screening committee should have access to management and employees of the organization to conduct its analysis. At this early stage, any interaction with company personnel should be confidential, restricted, and anonymous. Any requests for evidence (e.g., interviews, documents, e-mails, etc.) should be coordinated with legal counsel.

DOCUMENTING COMPLAINTS For any complaint that is considered to have merit, a separate claims report should be prepared independently from the claims log. A segregation of duties between the preparers of the claims log and the claims report will add another layer of internal control over claims handling. Figure 10.2 illustrates how complaints are logged, screened, and documented.

The claims report is a longer document based on an initial discussion with the whistle-blower conducted by a trained interviewer. This individual must have the ability to gather sufficient information and documentation during the initial interview so that the claim can move rapidly to the next phase of the process. A claims report includes details of the complaint, including but not limited to:

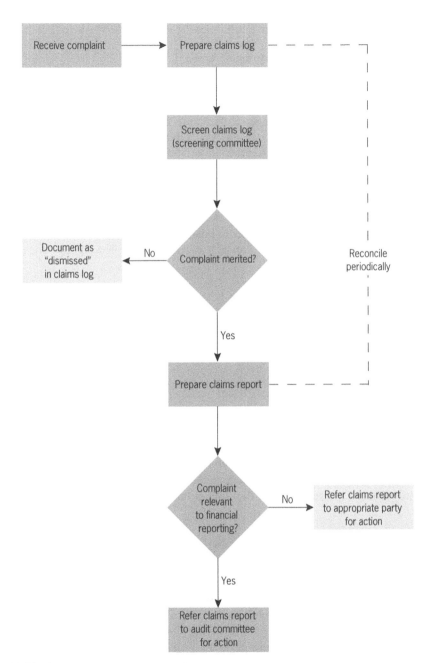

FIGURE 10.2 Receiving, Screening, and Documenting Claims

- Type of violation (i.e., legal, accounting, ethical, employment).
- Description of claim.
- Identification of parties/departments involved.
- Internal reporting hierarchy (e.g., managers, supervisors).
- Identification of others who might have knowledge about the claim.
- Whistle-blower authorization for disclosure (i.e., waiver of anonymity).
- Claim status (which will change as the claim moves through the handling process, e.g., Pending Action, No Action, Under Investigation, Withdrawn, Resolved, Dismissed).
- Comment sections for status updates as the claim moves through the process.

Depending on the circumstances, it may be appropriate to provide a copy of the report to the whistle-blower to ensure accuracy and to reinforce to the individual that the organization is serious about following up on claims.

Possible Governance Considerations

- Do company employees know how to receive and document whistle-blower complaints?
- Does the company screen claims to determine that they have merit and relevance for the audit committee?
- Are whistle-blower complaints logged in a standard form for appropriate follow-up?
- Are whistle-blower complaints documented in a standard form to facilitate processing?
- Does the company have procedures to ensure that whistle-blower claims are handled confidentially and anonymously?
- What assurances do directors and management have that complaints are appropriately reported to them in a timely manner?

Step 2: Analyze

After a whistle-blower complaint has been referred to it by the claims screening committee, the audit committee, assisted by legal counsel, should then perform a more in-depth analysis to determine the best course of action. An ideal way to make this assessment is to employ a standard for classifying complaints. The primary objective in classifying complaints is to determine which advisers will be required during the investigation phase. Consistently classifying whistle-blower complaints also speeds up and improves decision making. The MACH Process divides claims into classes based on two broad sets of factors:

TABLE 10.3 Whistle-Blower Criteria of MACH Process

Sensitivity factors	Materiality factors
• Involvement of board members, senior/executive officers • Violations of laws, rules, and regulations • Breaches of fiduciary duties • Regulatory issues that may cause inquiries or investigations • Material weaknesses in internal accounting controls • Potential for adverse public press	Dollar and/or percentage significance to: • Financial statements and related disclosures • Key operating metrics • Regulatory filings • Public disclosures • Incentive compensation • Covenants or operating agreements

1. *Sensitivity.* Those factors that, if disclosed, may cause significant harm to the company. They might include the alleged involvement of senior officers or directors, potential violations of laws, and asserted breaches of fiduciary duties, among others.
2. *Materiality.* Those factors that have the potential to significantly impact financial statements, regulatory filings, restrictive covenants, or incentive compensation, to name a few.

Examples of these two criteria are summarized in Table 10.3. The analysis of sensitivity and materiality will take thoughtful consideration of both qualitative (i.e., potential adverse impact) and quantitative (e.g., dollar amount) matters.

Possible Governance Considerations

- Does the company have an established method to determine the potential importance of a complaint?
- Does the company have predefined, consistent, and defensible standards for handling whistle-blower complaints?
- Does the audit committee have a mechanism to document the reasonable justification for courses of action taken to handle whistle-blower complaints?

Step 3: Investigate

How a whistle-blower complaint is investigated is directly dependent on how it is classified during the analysis phase. Specifically, the attributes of the complaint will determine which groups within and outside the organization may need to be involved in the investigation.

TABLE 10.4 Groups Involved in the Investigation Phase of a Whistle-Blower Complaint

	NS/NM	NS/M	S/NM	S/M
Management				
Human resources	•	•	•	•
Internal audit	•	•	•	•
Legal (internal or external)	•	•	•	•
Investor and public relations	•	•	•	•
Risk management		•	•	•
Information technology		•	•	•
External auditor		•	•	•
		•	•	•

NS = not sensitive; NM = not material; M = material; S = sensitive
• Recommended involvement   • Involvement depending on audit committee recommendation

APPOINTING THE INVESTIGATION TEAM The audit committee is responsible for investigating the claims referred to it, but it will want to bring others in as advisers, when appropriate. If a complaint is found to be neither sensitive nor material to the financial statements, the investigation can be assigned by the audit committee to uninvolved/disinterested management personnel and employees of the organization.

For any of the other three classifications of claims, the audit committee should consider the potential risk for an actual or perceived conflict of interest caused by the use of internal management personnel and employees to perform the investigation. At a minimum, the audit committee should engage independent, external legal counsel to oversee and supervise the investigation. In the case of sensitive but nonmaterial complaints, the audit committee will want to carefully consider whether certain internal groups need to be involved at all.

Table 10.4 presents one way of assigning different groups to the investigation based on the assessment of materiality and sensitivity during the analysis phase.

Depending on the situation, the audit committee may also want to bring in external advisers such as forensic accountants, specialty attorneys (e.g., regulatory, employment, insurance), bankers, insurance experts, and credit specialists to assist with an investigation. Preparing a plan, including identifying and qualifying experts, should be done as part of the MACH Process setup—not once a whistle-blower complaint has been tendered and the organization is under pressure to investigate. This will ensure that qualified resources are available when needed.

CONDUCTING THE INVESTIGATION The investigation should consist of all necessary procedures and actions to provide for the discovery, location, and procurement of sufficient facts to reach accurate conclusions. This will often require the use of specialized skills to locate, analyze, and preserve evidence. In addition, counterclaims by suspects are routine, and the company should prepare for this possibility.

Throughout this phase, the investigation team will need to determine who should receive sensitive information as it becomes available. The whistle-blower will want to know what happened to the complaint. The individuals implicated will need information to defend themselves. Others will also have a vested interest.

For example, in any investigation of a material whistle-blower complaint related to financial reporting, the external auditors will need to be involved and require information; however, they cannot be part of the actual investigation team for reasons of independence. Accordingly, they may "shadow" the investigation. In another case, if an investigation is sensitive in nature and there is a potential for "leaks," it may be necessary to involve the internal public relations team or an outside agency so that an appropriate communications plan can be implemented.

In general, it is advisable for legal counsel to direct the company as to who needs to receive what information, and when it should be released.

Possible Governance Considerations

- How will complaints that are not related to accounting, internal accounting controls, or auditing matters be handled by the organization?
- Has the audit committee developed a plan to use internal and external advisors to assist with whistle-blower complaints?
- Does the company have access to specialized skills to locate, analyze, and preserve whistle-blower investigative evidence?

Step 4: Resolve

The resolution of a complaint may impact only a very narrow portion of the company, as in the case of the handling of a single invoice or an expense report. However, a corrective action—for example, the termination of a senior executive officer for indiscretions or the restatement of previously issued financial statements—could be pervasive and far-reaching. Accordingly, the resolution of complaints requires the diligent and focused efforts of the audit committee and the parties designated by it to assist in completing corrective actions.

ISSUING A CORRECTIVE ACTION PLAN A corrective action plan is a set of anticipated procedures to be performed and actions to be followed to address and resolve a whistle-blower complaint. For example, the plan may call for the strengthening of an internal control, the rollout of a company-wide training program, a financial statement revision, or the termination of an employee. The corrective action plan should be formally approved and adopted by the audit committee. Before finalizing it, the audit committee will normally consult with management and external advisers to adequately consider company resource requirements and costs, as well as to address practical limitations.

IMPLEMENTING THE CORRECTIVE ACTION PLAN The audit committee should monitor the implementation of the corrective action plan until the matter is closed. Any material changes to the plan should be reviewed and approved by the audit committee. In some cases, the corrective action plan will call for steps to be taken before an investigation is complete. For example, if it appears there is a material weakness in internal controls, action—whether it is in the form of a policy amendment, a personnel change, or a restatement—must be taken immediately. Progress in the corrective action plan should be documented in the comments section of the claims report.

Possible Governance Considerations

- In practice, does the audit committee consult with management before adopting a corrective action plan in connection with a whistle-blower complaint?
- Is it company policy to have all corrective action plans for whistle-blower complaints approved by the audit committee?
- Are there procedures to ensure that changes to these plans are reported to the audit committee in a timely manner?
- What are the assurances that whistle-blower complaints are adequately and completely resolved?

Step 5: Report

Every action taken regarding a whistle-blower complaint will generate curiosity and will be closely monitored by interested parties. Whistle-blowers will expect timely reports on the status of their claims. Innocent suspects of wrongdoing want their absolution to be communicated promptly. Guilty parties need to be dealt with swiftly and decisively. The company's responsiveness signals that it takes these complaints seriously and is prepared to deal with them appropriately. Therefore, it is important to have well-defined communication and reporting protocols in place.

These protocols must respect privacy and confidentiality but still provide a reasonable level of information to parties inside, as well as outside, the organization. Management, directors, shareholders, and employees should be treated differently than regulators, auditors, and creditors. This may require the assistance of legal counsel, public relations professionals, and others to avoid liability for incomplete or inaccurate disclosures.

To provide the audit committee with assurance that all whistle-blower claims referred to it have been addressed, the claims log should be regularly reconciled to the claims reports and corrective action plans. As necessary, corrective action plans can be summarized and reported to the full board of directors, regulators, or other appropriate parties.

Because of privacy, anonymity, and confidentiality concerns, these documents and reports must be strictly secured, with proper chain of custody maintained, and the distribution and use of these items restricted. However, a system for capturing experiences from handling whistle-blower complaints can yield best practices for future decision making.

Possible Governance Considerations

- Does the company have policies for communicating whistle-blower investigations to interested parties?
- Does the company have an established communication protocol for those accused of wrongdoing by a whistle-blower?
- Does the company have internal controls over whistle-blower complaints to ensure that all complaints are handled?
- Does the company capture and share whistle-blower complaint investigation experiences to prevent future occurrences?

Step 6: Retain

Documents produced during the MACH Process represent evidence that should be preserved, protected, and retained in accordance with each company's document retention policies. As they may pertain to confidential matters reported by whistle-blowers afforded anonymity under the law, care must be taken to restrict access to hard-copy documents and to store and secure electronic data. This material also serves as a record of the audit committee's compliance with SOX and provides evidence that the organization is successfully addressing accounting, internal control, and auditing risk.

Possible Governance Considerations

- Do procedures exist to ensure whistle-blower complaints and related documents and data are appropriately secured, maintained, and retained in compliance with company policy?
- Does the company have systems to protect whistle-blower complaint investigative documents, findings and recommendations, corrective actions, and complaint resolutions from improper access?

TABLE 10.5 Whistleblower Complaint-Handling Performance Measures

Performance measures	

• Number of complaints
• Average number of complaints
  (e.g., per month)
• Complaints by entity, division,
  branch, store, or country
• Complaints by type of claim
• Number of investigations in
  process or completed
	• Average cost per complaint
	• Average cost per investigation
	• Ratio of complaints to type of outcome
	  (dropped vs. action necessary)
	• Ratio of complaints to:
	  − Sales
	  − Employee headcount
	  − Prior period averages

▪ Does the audit committee have a practice of documenting compliance with whistle-blower complaint-handling requirements mandated by SOX?

Monitoring the MACH Process

Once launched, the MACH Process must be monitored for compliance with the objectives and standards established by the audit committee. Compliance testing can also help identify opportunities for improvement in the MACH Process. In most cases, monitoring can be performed by internal auditors or by outsourcing the testing to a contractor. A stopgap measure may be to gauge compliance by using surveys completed by employees and other users.

However, without metrics, it will be difficult to know whether the MACH Process is a success. Metrics not only point to areas that need improvement; they also allow for trending and comparisons, both across the organization and against industry standards. The audit committee should identify performance metrics and operating benchmarks, as well as establish mechanisms for capturing this information. Table 10.5 lists some examples of metrics that can be used to gauge the performance of the MACH Process.

Reliable metrics will allow the audit committee to address such questions as:

▪ Are certain departments, groups, or individuals the target/source of more complaints than others?
▪ Has the incidence of complaints gone up over time? (This could be an indication that there is either greater usage of the process or that there is actually an increased number of incidents.)
▪ Are certain types of complaints on the rise? Are others decreasing?

Answers to these questions go beyond providing a performance report that sits on a shelf. They can be used to monitor and tighten the organization's control environment.

Possible Governance Considerations

- Have performance metrics been set up for the whistle-blower process?
- Have established benchmarks been gathered against which performance can be measured for the whistle-blower process?
- Does the company have the ability to collect information for periodic performance assessment of the whistle-blower process?
- Is a plan in place for testing compliance, monitoring performance, and analyzing trends in connection with the whistle-blower process?
- Does the company have systems to monitor its track record in swiftly responding to whistle-blower complaints?

Conclusion

SOX requires audit committees to fulfill their expanded responsibilities through the use of procedures to handle whistle-blower complaints about accounting, internal accounting controls, and auditing. This implies that a systematic process is needed to effectively perform these procedures. In the past, there has been little guidance available to audit committees and other governing bodies on how to set up such a process and create a repository for documenting complaints as they move through the system. Handling serious whistle-blower events is hard to prepare for—yet one misstep can have devastating effects. Companies and audit committees need to have an effective plan and process in place before whistleblower events arise.

This complaint-handling process that can be tailored to meet the needs of virtually any organization. The MACH Process is designed to ensure not only that venues exist for the gathering of whistle-blower complaints, but also that all complaints are documented, investigated, and addressed in the appropriate manner and that the process involves all necessary stakeholders. Furthermore, having this process in place will allow audit committees to demonstrate compliance with regulatory expectations and organizational objectives. The committee will also be able to monitor the success of the process, analyze trends, and identify areas for improvement.

In some organizations, the audit committee may choose to outsource its whistle-blower program to a third party that offers its own soup-to-nuts process for handling complaints. The MACH Process is not meant to replace such systems. Nevertheless, the guidelines summarized here should help audit committees evaluate the attributes of a vendor's whistle-blower services.

TABLE 10.6 To continuously improve a compliance program* a company should follow the practices of Assess/Prevent/Detect/Respond

Steps	Actions

Step 1 - Assess	• Self-assessment of corruption risks
	• Create risk profiles based on:
	  – Regions
	  – Governments
	  – Project size
	  – Project type (e.g., medical, natural resources, etc.)
	  – Agents/brokers/intermediaries involved
	  – Supply and distribution chains

Step 2 - Prevent	• Policies and procedures
	  – Business conduct guidelines
	  – Specific procedures for agents, gifts, and entertainment
	  – Checks/balances
	• Program communication
	  – Internal and external training
	• Training
	  – Targeted training programs for managers and operational personnel

Step 3 - Detect	• Compliance controls
	  – Risk management system
	  – Guidance and thresholds for escalation of compliance issues
	  – Integration with existing internal control (e.g., FCPA)
	  – Whistle-blower mechanisms
	• Forensic and part of standard audits
	  – Forensic audit function
	  – Audit review board

Step 4 - Respond	• Consequences for misconduct
	  – Policy of misconduct and sanctioning process
	• Global case tracking
	  – Tracking tool for compliance
	  – Internal and external reporting on compliance cases
	• Application of lessons learned
	  – Identify root causes and fix processes

*Additional compliance program information can be found at the web-sites of various anti-corruption and compliance-related organizations.

For the MACH Process, as for all processes, the "devil is in the details." The audit committee must consider the organization and the types of whistleblower complaints that are likely to surface. It must prepare for crisis situations by establishing relationships with a range of experts who will be available to assist should a situation arise. It must oversee training for individuals who will be responsible for documenting and investigating complaints. Finally, it must engender trust among those who wish to use the system, ensuring confidentiality to employees and a hearing to all who wish to file complaints (see Table 10.6). Ultimately, by establishing an effective whistleblower complaint-handling process, the organization will be able to identify and deal with those cases of fraud that have the greatest potential to harm the company's reputation and bottom line.

Appendix

Claim No.	Date Filed	Source of Claim		Claimant Contact Information (Note: information blank for internal anonymous claims)		Target of Claim (e.g., person, group, dept., division, etc.)	Dismissed	Action (Date)	
		Internal	External					Refer to Audit Committee	Refer to Other (Name)
2006 - 1	January 1, 2006	Hotline		**Personal: Anonymous**		Accounts receivable		January 15, 2006	
				Phone No.					
				Address					
				Address					
				Address					
				Fax No.					
				E-mail					
				Company: Any Company					
				Phone No.					
				Address					
				Address					
				Address					
				Fax No.					
				E-mail					
2006 - 2	March 1, 2006		Customer	**Personal: John Q. Customer**		Sales and marketing			To sales manager (Jack Doe) March 15, 2006
				Phone No.	123-456-7890				
				Address	123 Central Ave.				
				Address					
				Address	Anytown, State, Zip				
				Fax No.	123-456-7891				
				E-mail	jqcustomer@email.com				
				Company: Customer Company					
				Phone No.	234-567-8901				
				Address	456 Customer Lane				
				Address	Suite 123				
				Address	Anytown, State, Zip				
				Fax No.	234-567-8902				
				E-mail	www.customerco.com				

CHAPTER 11

Document Retention

William P. Olsen

Historically, document retention policies often have been overlooked as a best practice for organizations. Since passage of the Sarbanes-Oxley Act of 2002, however, document retention policies should be on the forefront of public—and private—companies' minds.

In fact, section 802 of the act, also known as the "Corporate and Criminal Fraud Accountability Act," spells out the criminal and civil penalties related to document destruction and improper document retention. Basically, the law states that anyone who alters, destroys, or conceals a record or document with the intent to impair the object's integrity or availability for use in an official proceeding will face criminal penalties.

The act also increased civil and criminal penalties for the following violations:

- Knowing destruction, alteration, or falsification of records in federal investigations and bankruptcy: fine and/or imprisonment up to 20 years.
- Knowing and willful destruction of corporate audit records in the retention period: fine and/or imprisonment up to 10 years.

Additional negative consequences for failing to have adequate procedures designed to prevent inappropriate document destruction include default judgments against a company, monetary sanctions, and a loss of public trust.

For private companies that are not governed by the act, taking a closer look at document retention policies is still an important consideration.

It makes good business sense for any company to properly maintain documents and stay current with federal and state regulations. Having a record retention policy not only helps an organization maintain the documents required by law, but also lends credibility to the importance it places on governance policies.

Create, Communicate, Monitor

The first step in addressing the act's requirements is to work with outside counsel to establish a document retention policy. After management and the board of directors finalize the policy, it must be communicated throughout the entire organization.

It is not an acceptable excuse after the fact to say that an employee did not understand that he or she was supposed to retain a certain document. An organization must be able to establish that the policy was clearly communicated to all levels of the organization.

To assure that the policy is being implemented correctly, companies should monitor compliance. Many companies are designating an individual—often someone from the board of directors—to be responsible for policy enforcement. He or she should also regularly monitor changes in law or regulation and, if necessary, take action to update the policy.

Reduce Risk through Technology

Essentially, a document retention policy is a risk management tool for the board of directors and management. When looking at how the company addresses document retention, a board might consider asking the following questions:

- Are e-mails backed up on a daily basis?
- Are documents being stored for proper retention periods?
- What technology/methods do we use to recover or reconstruct data?
- Does our technology have capabilities to extract data using specialized search techniques?

Key Elements of a Document Retention Policy

- Identify the types of documents covered under the policy.
- Develop a retention period for the different types of documents.
- Think through procedures for storing and disposing of documents.
- Establish a central depository and registry for retained records.
- Assign responsibility to someone in the organization for policy enforcement and monitoring new developments.
- Ensure that there are procedures in place to communicate the retention policy to all employees in the organization.

- Have mechanisms in place to stop destruction of all documents when notified of a pending government investigation.

Having the appropriate e-mail software package will save an organization a lot of money and heartache in the long run. Many e-mail software packages have a feature that allows searches to be performed to identify only those documents that contain information pertaining to certain selected names or terms. For example, if an organization receives a subpoena asking for information about a specific event or person, using a search engine to extract the right data is invaluable. Also, having the resources identified that are capable of properly imaging computer hard drives is essential when trying to maintain the integrity of the information. The days of searching through box after box should be over with the right technology in place.

Computer Crime

Computer-related crimes can be grouped into three categories that parallel the three stages of data processing: input tampering, throughput tampering, and output tampering. Input crimes involve the entry of false or fraudulent data into a computer, that is, data that have been altered, forged, or counterfeited—raised, lowered, destroyed, intentionally omitted, or fabricated. Input scams are probably the most common computer-related crimes, yet perhaps the easiest kind to prevent with effective supervision and controls (such as separation of duties and proper audit trails).

Throughput crimes require a knowledge of programming. The publicly reported cases of these crimes are far fewer than input crimes. Output crimes, such as theft of computer-generated reports and information files (customer mailing lists, research-and-development results, long-range plans, employee lists, secret formulas, etc.) seem to be increasing in this era of intense competition, particularly among high-technology manufacturers.

Among the publicly reported cases of computer crime, most have been the input and output type and have involved lower-level data processing clerks—entry clerks and computer operators. However, because throughput crimes are more difficult to detect, we cannot say that their number is exceeded by the other two types.

The Most Common Computer-Related Crimes

Whereas computer hacking (pranksters breaking into computers) has received most of the recent media attention, the most prevalent computer crime risk is at the higher management levels. The typical fraud involves overstating profits by fabrication of such data as sales, which are increased arbitrarily (sales booked before the sales transaction is completed), and the understatement of expenses, which are arbitrarily reduced or disguised as deferrals to the next accounting period. There are numerous variations on these two main themes—overstatement of sales and understatement of expenses. One of the more common ploys to overstate profits is to arbitrarily increase the ending inventory of manufactured goods or merchandise held for sale. That ploy results in understating the cost of goods sold and thereby increasing the net profit.

Manipulations of this type often require line executives and personnel in accounting and data processing capacities to conspire together. The pressure on executives for high performance grows each year. This same pressure that can cause management to "cook the books" is what often drives management to be willing to pay bribes to obtain proprietary information in order to be more competitive on bids, and why government officials will pay bribes to get the competitive edge on foreign competition.

The Value of Stored Data

With the advent of computers, a new form of asset has been created: the data held in the computer. The intellectual property maintained in computers can be extremely valuable to foreign governments and foreign competition. Other, more intangible assets include valued or confidential programs, scientific data files, confidential financial information, personnel records, client lists, and so on.

Companies will greatly benefit from strong adherence to retention policies, and the governance of such policies, for documents and information in hard or electronic formats.

CHAPTER 12

Information Security

Intellectual Property Theft Is Often the Result of Government Corruption

William P. Olsen

In today's global economy, the most valuable asset for most organizations is their intellectual property—their knowledge. How effectively an organization manages and protects its knowledge will directly impact its ability to compete and grow. Most forms of intellectual property are subject to specific legal protections that are publicly filed and widely known. Legal protections such as patents, copyrights, trademarks, trade dress, and service marks are routinely utilized to enforce intellectual property rights and provide organizations a reasonable degree of certainty that such information and ideas will be protected. These protections also provide a means of obtaining redress through legal action. However, a large and growing segment of intellectual property—trade secrets—is often unrecognized and routinely left unprotected. Many organizations do not appreciate the amount and types of intellectual property they have, let alone know how much of it consists of trade secrets. In fact, many do not really appreciate the importance of the trade secrets they possess. This is troubling in light of recent FBI figures that place the cost of losses due to economic espionage in the multimillions.

Intellectual property is essentially all proprietary information that an organization may possess so long as this information is being protected. Trade secrets are defined by the Economic Espionage Act of 1996 (EEA) to include all forms of information if the owner of the information has taken reasonable measures to keep the information secret, and if the information derives independent economic value from not being generally known or being readily discernible through proper means by the public. The EEA provides protection for trade secrets and provides for criminal penalties for those who knowingly and without authorization appropriate, copy, destroy, deliver, convey, receive, or possess the trade secrets of another. In addition, many states have similar statutes that have both civil and criminal provisions. Thus, organizations that do not take *reasonable steps* to protect their proprietary trade secrets are not only risking loss of the same through theft or industrial espionage, they may be giving up what little legal protections exist for trade secrets. Bribery by government officials to obtain trade secrets is very common in the global marketplace and a huge risk for organizations, as the financial impact can be severe.

A comprehensive program to identify, classify, and protect trade secrets is vitally important in this information age. Failure to do so can cause an organization to lose market share, lose valuable technology and information assets, reduce the organization's capacity to compete, and ultimately drive it out of business. However, no one program is correct for every organization. The needs, culture, strategic vision, and physical aspects of an organization all affect the controls that should be implemented. The key word in protecting trade secrets is *reasonable*. Organizations should strive to implement *reasonable* controls to protect their proprietary information.

It is necessary to strike a balance between security and usability, for the most secure information in the world is of no use if no one can access it and take advantage of it. A risk-based approach is often the best course of action to take. Such a process starts with identifying, assessing, and evaluating key risks to an organization's proprietary information. The process also entails identifying what proprietary information an organization has, where it is located, and who has access to it. Once this information has been identified, its relative importance needs to be evaluated.

A comprehensive program needs coordination among numerous areas of responsibility and control. Coordination among physical security, information systems security, human resources, document management and control, legal counsel, and other risk management departments must be successfully implemented in order for an effective program to work. If an overall approach is not taken, a false sense of security may be instilled, and the time and resources spent on tightening some areas will be wasted.

Understanding the threat is the first step in developing effective measures to protect intellectual property. The threat comes from both internal and external sources. Competitors, foreign governments, gatherers of competitive intelligence, disgruntled employees, insiders, intruders, contract workers, maintenance/service staff, terminated employees, industrial spies, and dishonest employees all pose significant risks. Knowing and understanding how these threats gain access to information and discovering what security weaknesses exist is instrumental in developing effective countermeasures.

Information Security Audit

In order to effectively manage and control its information capital, every organization needs to know what trade secrets or proprietary information it owns and where this information is maintained. Each organization then needs to determine whether this information is being adequately protected. A trade secret audit is the first step in effectively managing and protecting proprietary information. Such an audit entails not only identifying those items that are trade secrets, but also entails a comprehensive analysis of the protections currently in place to secure such items. Effective audits will reveal the weaknesses within an organization's controls. This audit will also enable an organization to evaluate its proprietary information. Further, valuation of the organization's trade secrets or proprietary information can be crucial if an organization has to resort to legal action to enforce its rights.

Classification of Information

Once an organization has identified the trade secrets it owns and where these assets reside within the organization, it needs to classify them in order of importance to the organization's mission. Those items that have been identified as mission critical must be afforded the utmost protection. The organization then needs to identify those items that, while still proprietary, are of little or no consequence. Such items will be afforded a minimal level of protection. Any classification scheme can contain very few levels or many levels, depending on the needs of the organization. A simple four-tiered classification scheme might contain the following levels:

1. *Classified.* Mission-critical information that is to be afforded the utmost protection. Only those employees directly involved in the development or actual use of such information with an absolute need to know will be allowed access. Access to such information is to be closely monitored, and an appropriate audit trail will be maintained to track any access. Such information is not to be disclosed to anyone outside the core group of those individuals who have been authorized to access it.
2. *Confidential.* Access strictly limited to those employees or groups of employees who have an actual need to know.
3. *Sensitive.* The information is for the use of authorized employees on a broader organizational scale. Such information still should not be disclosed to nonauthorized employees or outsiders.
4. *Unrestricted.* Such information contains public information or other information that is of little consequence to the organization's proprietary property.

No single classification scheme will be correct for any particular organization. The needs of each organization must be considered and evaluated before any such scheme can be implemented. An information security audit will identify the various amounts and degrees of proprietary information and will provide the requisite insight into what classification scheme will be appropriate.

Access to documentation and other information must also be prioritized. This procedure ties into the systems control procedures. There are several levels on which prioritization may be based. The first of these is on an organization-wide level. Criteria, such as which executives or employees need complete access to any and all information, need to be considered. Information that needs to be accessed on an organization-wide basis, so-called unrestricted or sensitive information, needs to be identified. Access within a department or functional unit also needs to be restricted in certain circumstances. For all information marked as classified, this means a truly eyes-only basis. Only those individuals that are specifically working on a particular project should have access. The access prioritization needs to be developed subsequent to the information prioritization process being completed.

Division of Responsibilities and Duties Is an Effective Strategy in Protecting Trade Secrets

For information that is extremely confidential or classified, a division of responsibilities will reduce the risk that an entire process, procedure, or strategy will be misappropriated or otherwise accessed in an unauthorized manner. This will also ensure that no one person will possess all the information or knowledge, thus reducing the risk of loss.

Information Security Control Officers or Custodians

Information security control officers or custodians can be identified within the organization to ensure that access is limited to those who need access to the information.

This person can be assigned the task of granting requests for access to the various levels of information. This person should also be given the responsibility of monitoring situations in which unauthorized access has been attempted or obtained and then make the necessary notifications within the organization to carry out any actions necessary to protect proprietary information and enforce security policies.

Use of Confidential or Proprietary Markings

All confidential information should be prominently denoted as such. Hard copies of documents, drawings, diagrams, and the like shall be marked as confidential or proprietary trade secrets. Each page should be so marked. Items that are stored electronically also should openly carry the appropriate designations. For those items considered to be mission critical, warnings should be in place indicating that the copying, downloading, or other means of accessing the item is not permitted without authority from the custodian of that particular document or the trade secret control office.

Document Destruction

Just as important as how an organization retains its records is how it destroys its records. Trash receptacles, dumpsters, or other open areas are a prime source for industrial spies and gatherers of competitive intelligence. *Any* document that contains proprietary information or trade secrets should be shredded prior to disposal. This includes drafts, amendments, revisions, and even handwritten notes. If employees are in the habit of working from home or other off-site locations, the same level of care should be employed at these locations. If shredding is not practical at such locations, the documents should be retained and shredded at the organization. Hotels and other off-site locations can pose their own set of problems. Proprietary information should never be left unattended in a hotel room or other nonsecure location. Notes or other documents containing sensitive information should be kept under close control. Strict control should be exercised over drafts of documents such as proposals and bids. Often, crucial information that is not much different from the final information is contained in the document.

Education and Training

All staff must be sensitized to the nature of trade secrets and proprietary information. Often, employees are unaware of what constitutes intellectual property, let alone steps to protect it. Effective training in this regard is a necessary step in creating an atmosphere in which trade secrets can remain secret. All employees should be required to sign non-disclosure forms indicating that they understand what proprietary information is and their responsibility in protecting such from disclosure. This must be done at all levels of the organization. Training must be updated and must occur on a regular basis.

Background Checks

Organizations should consider conducting background investigations on employees in sensitive positions, employees with access to proprietary information, and, at a minimum, employees in the executive ranks or other high-level positions within the organization. Such investigations should include, at a minimum, data available from public sources concerning liens, judgments, bankruptcies, Uniform Commercial Code (UCC) filings, Securities and Exchange Commission (SEC) actions, as well as publication checks. Criminal background checks should also be considered for those individuals who will have access to highly confidential information or who will be in a position of trust. In any event, the employment history and educational history should be verified on all employees.

Temporary employees pose a special problem to organizations. In today's workplace, even temporary employees are given access to sensitive information without so much as a confidentiality agreement in place. It is very easy for practitioners of industrial espionage to place such employees in organizations or to gain access to and influence such employees. Temporary employees should be limited in their level of access to proprietary information if information regarding their background is not obtained.

Confidentiality Agreements

Confidentiality agreements are one of the most effective tools in raising employees' awareness as to the importance that proprietary information plays in the organization. More importantly, it is a reasonable step and can be a powerful tool if the organization ever needs to take action against an employee or other insider that misappropriates or otherwise exercises unauthorized control over a trade secret. All employees should execute confidentiality agreements upon hiring and once again each year at their annual review. This will serve as a regular reminder to employees that they must do their utmost to protect the knowledge assets of the organization.

In those jurisdictions where noncompete clauses are enforceable, such confidentiality agreements can be an effective way to protect your organization from further damage by a departing employee. Agreements restricting the hiring away of coemployees by former employees, vendors, clients, or joint venture partners can also help to limit the loss of trade secrets.

Employee Orientation

All new employees should be thoroughly briefed on the importance of trade secrets to the organization's mission. Likewise, all incoming employees shall be notified not to bring others' trade secrets into the new organization. Such activity is happening with more and more frequency, as the job market becomes more and more transient. The use of trade secrets that are the property of another organization should not be tolerated. Organizations should avoid even the inadvertent use of such information. A strong statement that such information will not be utilized and that such behavior will not be tolerated will assist the organization immensely in the event of an accusation that proprietary information has been used in this manner.

Even though the organization should have a strong policy statement against using the proprietary information of others, the organization should determine whether new hires have executed or are otherwise covered by any preexisting confidentiality agreements. If so, extra care should be taken so as not to put the organization or the employee in a position where the agreement may be violated. Such steps also would be useful if the organization is accused of obtaining or attempting to obtain proprietary information. The organization can point to the steps or efforts taken should any disputes arise.

Separation Plans

The organization should have a plan in place describing how to best protect its information when employees leave the organization. Once management gains knowledge that an employee is leaving the organization, it should take appropriate steps to limit the vulnerability of its information assets. Reacquiring sensitive or classified items is of utmost importance. If employees are in the habit of taking work or other information home, management should ensure that all items are recovered. Departing employees' access to systems, documents, and other proprietary information should be monitored to prevent improper or unauthorized access, copying, or transmittal.

Upon separation from the organization, all departing employees should be provided with a copy of the previously executed confidentiality agreement that is in effect. As part of the exit interview, the employee should be reminded of his or her obligations under the agreement. In addition, any such agreements can be sent to the new employer, if known, in a nonthreatening educational manner. This will put the new employer on notice that any proprietary information the new employee may bring with him or her could result in a violation of the agreement as well as criminal law. This practice also goes a long way to creating a record to establish knowledge on the part of the violating organization should such misuse occur.

The organization should have a plan in place for unexpected employee separations. When employees are in the process of leaving or have accepted positions elsewhere, organizations are at increased risk to loss of proprietary information. If management receives information concerning the imminent departure of an employee, steps should be taken to ensure that no loss will occur. Any access to classified, confidential, or sensitive documents should be curtailed, if not totally eliminated. If it is known that the employee is leaving for a direct competitor, such access should be revoked immediately; logical access to all computer systems should be removed (i.e., user should not be able to log on to any computer with a user ID and password), and any physical access to facilities should be barred. In many cases, it may be prudent to immediately remove all access to systems, sites, and facilities as soon as management receives knowledge of an employee's impending departure.

Physical Security

Limited Access to Facility

Appropriate degrees of physical access control should be implemented at all locations, consistent with the type of information and the risks to physical loss. This is a crucial part of any comprehensive trade secret program, for even the best practices and systems security measures will be ineffective if physical access controls are substandard. A balance, however, needs to be struck between security and usability.

Limited Access within Facility

Access to certain areas within a facility often needs to be limited to those with an absolute need to have such access. Although many organizations need a free flow of personnel and information throughout their facilities, those areas that contain the more sensitive information, documents, and systems need greater protection.

Visitors' activities need to be closely monitored and escorts should be utilized in areas where access to sensitive information is possible. In those areas where information needing the highest protection is located, visitors should be denied all access. Use of items such as blackboards, whiteboards, or other media that are easily viewed should be carefully monitored if the facility has visitors or other outsiders who may gain access. Sensitive information should not be left displayed in open view during breaks. At the conclusion of any meeting, such information should be erased or removed from the open areas.

Many organizations routinely allow outside parties access to their facilities. Many times, this access is allowed unfettered. Outsiders like the coffee vendor, photocopier repair person, interior landscape personnel, and others are often allowed access to facilities. This access should be limited or eliminated in areas where mission-critical information is developed or stored. Cleaning personnel also pose another problem. They often have access to facilities after hours when there are few employees around. Such persons can easily access sensitive material or information that may be left in unsecured locations. Careless handling of documents, system user IDs, and passwords to systems can lead to the loss of proprietary information. Controls should be in place to limit access to areas that contain trade secrets or other sensitive information.

The introduction or removal of items such as computers, computer media, recording devices, cameras, film, and so on also should be restricted for those facilities or areas wherein the most sensitive information resides.

ID Badges

In those cultures where appropriate, ID badges can be an effective method of preventing or deterring unauthorized access to a facility. Of course, the workforce needs to be educated to the importance of wearing badges and of challenging those individuals who are not displaying badges. If ID badges are utilized, all visitors should be required to wear one prominently displayed. Strict control should be exercised over all badges to prevent misappropriation.

Systems Security

The proliferation of computer technology, coupled with the increased use of the Internet and e-mail, has made it easier than ever to misappropriate proprietary trade secrets. Where once thieves and industrial spies had to physically carry documents or other information out of a facility, they can now do so through a few keystrokes from a remote location. Similarly, a disgruntled or dishonest employee can gain access to and transmit sensitive data from within an organization quickly and easily. Systems security is an integral part of any trade secret protection program. Many of these best practices are currently being employed to a certain degree in many organizations. However, they are rarely implemented as part of a total organization approach to trade secret protection. As part of any trade secret audit, the existence or efficacy of such controls needs to be verified and tested.

Ownership of and Access to Information

Each organization should place a statement of privacy or other form of notification on their systems that informs each user upon start-up that all activity on the system may be monitored. The statement should further inform each user that all information contained on any system, storage device server, and so on is the property of the organization. It is important to establish this clearly and regularly. The use of such notification will obviate privacy claims that employees may make with respect to documents, e-mail, or other data contained on the organization's systems. Such a notification will ease the organization's ability to freely obtain data and other information from its systems during any investigation or audit.

Authorization

Each organization needs to develop a system whereby access to information is controlled and monitored. The ability to access, modify, download, print, or delete documents should be controlled on a system-wide basis. Authorization to access information should be on a need-to-know basis. Access should be separated by department, unit, or across the organization. Such authorization should be based on responsibilities and job classifications. For example, an organization may have many departments and many servers or systems. An employee of an accounts payable department does not necessarily need access to the research-and-development system or the information contained therein. However, employees of the sales department of a manufacturer may need to have access to certain information in the production department's system or area. Even within a department, levels or degrees of access need to be considered and prioritized. Not every employee needs to have access to all information.

A privacy statement that indicates that all information on the system belongs to the organization and is subject to monitoring can help relieve concerns about privacy, while at the same time remind the employees that the information belongs to the organization. This effectively puts the employee on notice of his or her responsibilities each time that employee gains access to the system.

Passwords

Use of passwords is a well-known but often overlooked security measure. Power-on passwords, system passwords, server passwords, and firewall passwords are simple yet effective ways to provide a basic level of security to proprietary information that may reside in an organization's system.

Documents of the higher-sensitivity classifications should be password protected themselves to further limit their unauthorized access. In addition, system passwords need to be utilized and updated regularly. Employees should be prohibited from sharing passwords with other employees. Similarly, employees should be discouraged from writing down or otherwise recording their passwords in locations that are easily accessible.

Biometric Devices

In those highly sensitive areas or for situations where access to information must be severely restricted, the use of biometric devices can prove to be an excellent method of guarding against unauthorized access to systems and facilities. Such devices ensure that only the authorized user will gain access to the restricted area. Examples of such devices are fingerprint readers, handprint readers, and face recognition technology. These devices reduce the risk of unauthorized access through theft or misappropriation of passwords, as they rely on an individual's unique physical characteristics as an access control.

Usage Records

Usage records, exception reporting, or other audit trail methodologies should be in place so that if someone gains unauthorized access to a system, a trail or other record of the event will be kept. Such information is crucial for litigation, investigative, and auditing purposes. Adequate audit trails can allow an organization to monitor excessive downloads, printing runs, e-mail usage, and other indications that an employee may be accessing information in an unauthorized manner or plans to make unauthorized use of the information.

Encryption

E-mail or other electronic communication of confidential information should be encrypted to prevent the unauthorized reading of such information. Due to the nature of the Internet, transmissions are easily intercepted and can even be monitored and read. Encryption technology can prevent someone from reading your organization's communication of confidential information or documents. The document classification system is a good starting point in developing a good encryption policy. The usage of such technology should be monitored and enforced to ensure the protection of information.

Firewalls

Firewalls are devices that act as a suit of armor for a computer network. While not infallible, they provide basic protection from unauthorized personnel seeking access. All computer systems should have a series of firewalls to prevent unauthorized access to the system. Firewalls are effective but must be continuously monitored so as not to allow for a false sense of security.

Intrusion Detection

Intrusion detection is an effective complement to firewalls in detecting and controlling unauthorized access. Intrusion detection devices can be placed both inside and outside firewalls. These devices do exactly what their name suggests. They detect instances when unauthorized persons gain access to a system. Thus, if someone were able to penetrate a firewall, an intrusion detection device could detect this and alert the system administrator so that an appropriate response could be made.

Anti-Virus Protection

Although viruses are not a threat with regard to the misappropriation of trade secrets, they do pose a substantial threat to information. State-of-the-art virus protection systems should be implemented to ensure that an organization's data and other information are not lost through destruction or deletion. Any system that has access to the Internet or other systems should have virus protection in place.

Dedicated Systems

An extreme security step an organization can take is to have a dedicated system that is totally self-contained with no outside access available. Although such a system is hardly usable and makes information sharing impossible, it helps ensure that no one can obtain unauthorized access to the organization's most sensitive information.

Media Tracking

Media tracking refers to monitoring and controlling the use and access to devices such as CD-ROMs, disks, tapes, and the like. Media tracking can be employed to prevent unauthorized copying of information contained on the organization's computer systems.

Sniffers

Sniffers are devices that can monitor traffic on a system for certain words, phrases, or other criteria. They can be an effective tool in monitoring the distribution of sensitive information through e-mail. For example, sniffers can be placed on a system to monitor certain key words that may be contained in trade secrets that a dishonest employee may be attempting to transmit to an unauthorized person via e-mail.

Modems

Computers should not be left on during nonwork hours and in no event should connections through modems be left open and unattended. The use of external modems should be strictly limited, and all modems should be registered with the information technology (IT) department.

Disposal of Computer Equipment

The sale or disposal of unwanted computer equipment can pose significant risks to the security of information. Prior to discarding or disposing of unwanted or obsolete computers, servers, storage devices, electronic media, and any other hardware devices capable of storing data, all data on any such device should be thoroughly erased by appropriate means.

Contingency Plan

Organizations should have contingency plans in place for responding to system emergencies. Such a plan would require periodic backups of data, allow for continuing operations in the event of an emergency, and have disaster recovery plans.

E-Mail Policy

With the proliferation of the Internet and the use of e-mail, organizations are at greater risk for the unauthorized electronic transmission of proprietary information. Although many organizations currently have a general policy concerning the misuse or conversion of organizational property, many do not have a policy specific to e-mail. Many organizations that do have e-mail policies do not enforce them. As a result, the use of e-mail for nonorganizational (i.e., personal) purposes can flourish. This can also allow the unauthorized or illegal distribution of trade secrets. Each organization should have a simple, easy-to-apply e-mail policy. At a minimum, the use of e-mail for confidential communications should be restricted to those situations in which encryption is being utilized. This will enable the organization to have a level of comfort in knowing that unauthorized persons will not read confidential or sensitive information.

If an organization has decided that it will allow its employees to utilize e-mail for personal purposes, it is even more imperative that its use is monitored. Steps such as using sniffers and other devices to monitor e-mail traffic can be applied to deter the use of e-mail to send proprietary information out of the organization.

E-mail can often be a source of unauthorized access or other threats to an organization's information. One important step in protecting against this threat is to instruct employees not to open e-mail from unknown persons or entities. There are a significant number of viruses and other executable programs that can cause damage to systems or may provide the means for someone to access the system at a later date. At a minimum, computer viruses can erase months' or years' worth of work if backups are not maintained. Systems should prompt employees to verify or determine who they are receiving e-mail from prior to opening it. An effective e-mail policy needs to be coupled with effective document and record-retention policies.

- Are e-mails backed up on a daily basis?
- Are electronic documents being stored for property retention periods?
- What technology/methods do we use to recover or reconstruct data?
- Does our technology have capabilities to extract data using specialized search techniques?

Internet Policy

Like e-mail, Internet access can pose difficult problems to organizations that wish to effectively control the unauthorized use of or access to proprietary information. Both Internet access and e-mail pose the problem of opening up an organization's computer systems to unauthorized access. They also pose problems arising from insiders utilizing easy means of transmitting large amounts of information extremely quickly. An effective Internet policy can limit some of the problems that exist on the Internet today. Limiting access to certain sites can be an effective method of limiting exposure to viruses and other damaging programs. Capturing each user's history can be an effective control, as this retains a record of the sites an employee has accessed. This can later assist during an investigation of the theft or misappropriation perpetrated by an insider.

Solicitations for Information

All employees, from receptionists to senior executives, should take care when responding to inquiries from outsiders such as researchers, sales persons, or others who may solicit information over the phone or other forms of communication. For instance, a call to the IT department seeking information regarding what systems the company uses may be from a legitimate vendor. It also could be from someone who is seeking information to facilitate unauthorized access to the organization's system. Trade shows are also a favorite place for competitors and industrial spies seeking information. Sales representatives need to take extra care not to reveal proprietary information. Effective training regarding the methods utilized by gatherers of competitive intelligence can help reduce these risks. Each employee should be made aware of such practices, as well as what to do when such inquiries are made.

Seminar/Tradeshow/Off-Site Meetings Policy

Off-site meetings can often prove to be great sources of vulnerability to the protection of proprietary information. Many employees are not sensitive to the risks when they get to an off-site location. However, the risks are often increased, for the organization does not have as much control over access and other security issues. The use of wireless microphones in meetings in which critical trade secret information is going to be discussed should be limited. Portable scanners can pick up the signals from such microphones. Just as you would not invite a competitor into a closed-door strategy meeting, neither should wireless microphones be utilized when discussing highly confidential information.

Close control should be placed over any documents that are distributed that contain trade secrets or other sensitive information. Such materials should not be left in plain view during breaks. Any unwanted or unused documents should be turned in and maintained until such time that they can be properly disposed of. Similarly, caterers, waiters, and other staff should be kept out of meetings during times in which highly confidential information is to be discussed.

At meetings off site, many times employees can be careless with documents and other information that are utilized at such meetings. Control should be exercised over such items during breaks and at the conclusion of meetings. All unnecessary items should be disposed of in accordance with the document retention/destruction policy.

Employees who attend trade shows or seminars should be trained to exercise caution when discussing issues that approach or touch on strategic or proprietary issues. Many times, organizations send people to such functions with instructions to gather as much information about as many competitors as they can. Many of the same approaches and policies that are applied at an organization's facilities can be utilized off-site as well.

Joint Venture/Vendor/Subcontractor Procedures

Joint ventures, mergers, acquisitions, reorganizations, outsourcing, strategic partnerships, vendors, subcontractors, and other similar relationships all have significant implications with regard to an organization's proprietary information. While sharing of certain information must occur in order for such arrangements to work, steps can be taken to help limit unauthorized access to trade secrets. First, confidentiality agreements must be executed between all parties to these arrangements. If access to systems is to be shared, such access should be limited only to those areas of mutuality. Likewise, physical access should be limited to those areas that are necessary to carrying out the objectives of the arrangement. How information that was shared during the relationship is to be treated upon termination of the venture should be carefully spelled out.

Any agreements, contracts, or memoranda of understanding should include language requiring that each partner will afford the same level of protection to each other's trade secrets that the owner of the trade secrets currently provides. This applies to every aspect of the trade secret protection program. The agreement should also give the organization the right to verify that these minimal protections are in place and are monitored. Employees of any partners should sign agreements protecting all partners. Employees of all entities that will be affected should be educated as to the sensitivities of all information that is to be shared.

Organizations should notify all affected employees of the existence of any partnering arrangements and any limitations they impose. The organization needs to inform its employees which trade secrets are subject to the partnering arrangement. The organization also needs to inform its employees which specific employees of the partner may have access to which secrets. Employees also should be sensitized to the importance of not discussing, sharing, or otherwise carelessly allowing access to information that is not the subject of the venture. Often, employees become complacent and discuss issues unrelated to the arrangement. Remember that today's partner may be tomorrow's competitor! Contractual provisions should be inserted into any agreement, indicating the minimal protections of trade secrets that will be in place.

Contractual Provisions with End Users

Proprietary information in the possession of others represents one of the largest single risks of loss of such information. Failure to take reasonable steps to protect this information when in the possession of others may cause the information to lose its trade secret status. Every organization that may receive such information in the normal course of business should be required to sign an agreement indicating that it recognizes that such information is confidential and that it shall be afforded the requisite protections.

Action Plans

Defensive Plan

Procedures must be established for the swift investigation of allegations of the misappropriation or unauthorized use of intellectual property. The organization should then initiate an investigation to identify how this information was received and by whom. If the organization determines that its trade secrets have been accessed in an unlawful or unauthorized manner, it should follow its action plan to resolve the issue as expeditiously as possible.

From a defensive position, plans should be in place to cease the unauthorized use of the trade secret of another as soon as such use comes to the management's attention. If such information has been utilized, it should be immediately isolated so that no further dissemination occurs, and removed from all files, storage areas, and records to guard against action being taken against the organization. It also should be isolated from all areas so that you will be able to prove that other nonoffending actions, products, and development were completed independently of this information.

Legal Action Plan

As time is of the essence in misappropriation/unauthorized use of trade secrets cases, a legal action plan should be in place to allow the organization to respond quickly. Competent counsel that specialize in intellectual property should be identified, and arrangements should be made to utilize counsel in the event of the unauthorized taking or use of the organization's proprietary information. Such counsel should be familiar with the organization's systems and controls as well as the nature of the organization's business so that he or she may quickly respond. Counsel should be provided with any confidentiality or noncompete agreements that are in effect.

As part of the legal action plan, consideration should be given as to how and even whether to enforce trade secrets through litigation. Consultation with appropriate legal counsel should be undertaken concerning the risks of further disclosure of trade secrets during litigation.

Information Technology Action Plan

As more organizations rely on technology in conducting their everyday affairs, the use of such technology to improperly gain access to the organization's proprietary information increases. During the trade secret audit, the IT department should have gained a thorough understanding of where the information is kept and what protections have been put in place. Audit trails and other records must be maintained and saved for further analysis.

Sometimes this will be the only information available to investigators and attorneys as they try to resolve breaches. The plan should be carried out at the highest levels in the IT department due to the sensitive nature of such investigations.

Physical Action Plan

If it is determined that a lapse in physical security has led to the loss of proprietary information, the corporate security department must be notified immediately. Responsible personnel should be identified to conduct a thorough review to determine if the access or loss was the result of a breach of security or whether it was the result of inadequate controls in the first place. A review of the security procedures currently in place must be undertaken to prevent similar losses in the future.

International Protection Issues

In many foreign jurisdictions, there are few or no legal protections afforded to trade secrets. Extra care should be taken when conducting business in such areas. It is just as important to implement a comprehensive protection plan in those jurisdictions as it is in the United States.

Information Security Policy

Organizations should establish trade secret or proprietary information security policies. Such policies should delineate the importance of trade secrets to the organization's mission as well as each employee's obligation to protect this information. Such a policy should, at a minimum, indicate that:

- Information is vital to the economic well-being of the organization.
- Every cost-effective effort will be made to ensure the confidentiality, control, integrity, authenticity, availability, and utility of the organization's information.
- Protecting the confidentiality, control, integrity, authenticity, availability, and utility of the organization's information is a priority for all employees at all levels; confidentiality, control, integrity, authenticity, availability, and utility of the proprietary information of other organizations will not be violated.
- All information processing facilities belonging to the organization will be used for authorized organization purposes.

CHAPTER 13

Anti–Money Laundering
The USA PATRIOT Act
William P. Olsen and Kelly Gentenaar

The passage of the USA PATRIOT Act ("Patriot Act") a consequence of September 11, 2001, played a crucial part in increasing the awareness of money laundering and the financing of terrorism. The act was, in part, passed to facilitate the prevention, detection, and prosecution of international money laundering and the financing of terrorism. However, prior to 2001, world leaders and governing organizations had already recognized money laundering as an increasingly devastating consequence of the globalization of the world's financial network.

The fundamental idea behind regulations provided by the Patriot Act and the Bank Secrecy Act is to catch criminals at their most vulnerable point in the money laundering cycle, that is, at the time funds are introduced into the financial network. Financial institutions act as the gatekeepers for entry into the financial network.

As the world's financial network has become increasingly globalized, the emphasis in the anti–money laundering (AML) community has come to include smaller institutions in addition to the larger and more international institutions that have traditionally been the focus of these global concerns. The AML regulations have changed over time because those involved in money laundering have adjusted to the current regulatory environment. These individuals constantly adapt to regulations and search out new means to continue their illegal activity. Often, certain industries or types of organizations of industries can, due to their size, give the appearance of getting less scrutiny from the regulators. Given the recent increases in regulatory requirements for other businesses, such as credit card companies and investment brokers, community banks could become targeted by these individuals because of that perception.

All entities designated as a "financial institution" in the Bank Secrecy Act required under the Patriot Act to establish an AML program. This program should be designed to be appropriate for the size of the organization and should utilize a risk-based approach for the areas of products and services, customers, geographic areas, and transaction types. The AML program needs to be documented and approved by the board of directors and should describe internal policies, procedures, and controls for AML regulatory compliance. Employees on the front lines and throughout the organization must be made aware of the "red flags" of money laundering and must be trained to know the current regulatory reporting requirements, including currency transaction reports (CTRs) and suspicious activity reports (SARs). Employee training must be tracked and documented.

Additionally, management and the board of directors must approve the implementation of the program and a compliance officer needs to be designated to oversee the function of the program. Once the program is in place, ongoing monitoring to ensure compliance is necessary. The organization must establish an independent testing function for all aspects of the program. Issues and concerns found during the testing and during the applicable regulator examinations must be followed up and addressed by management.

Current State of AML in the Global Marketplace

The organic unification of financial markets in our globalized economy has, for a long time, fostered an environment well suited for money laundering and terrorist financing. However, in the post-9/11 world, domestic and international agencies and organizations have made great strides in working together to combat the threat money laundering poses to the global economy. Due to the inconsistencies of legal structures from an international perspective and the complexity of the regulatory environment domestically, these efforts to create a unified front have been met with challenges. Therefore, the current state of AML can be characterized by two contradictory forces: unification in policy and inconsistency in application.

Although there is no global AML regime, international member groups such as the Financial Action Task Force (FATF) and the Egmont Group of Financial Intelligence Units (FIUs) are gaining recognition in the arena of AML as leaders within the international arena. The FATF has the role of providing recommendations to member countries. These recommendations are considered the starting point of any AML program. FATF also established the Non-Cooperative Countries and Territories (NCCT) list. The NCCT is a list of countries whose AML programs do not meet the 40 recommendations put out by FATF with the formal de-listing of Myanmar in October 2006, The FATF has refocused the NCCT process to that of monitoring as there are no remaining countries listed on the NCCT. Further improvements were made in conjunction with FATF's 40 recommendations; in 2004, FATF published nine special recommendations for terrorist financing. In addition to the new recommendations, the Republic of Korea was admitted as an observer to the FATF. This is showing even more unity in the fight against money laundering and terrorist financing. In June 2006, the plenary session of the Egmont Group met in Cyprus to discuss sending Egmont representatives to work with Interpol and the Wolfsburg Group. Furthermore, Egmont committee members met with representatives of FATF-Style Regional Bodies (FSRBs) to help determine the roles and responsibilities of various agencies in combating money laundering and terrorist financing. All these advancements are solidifying the fact that international unity is needed in order to properly combat money laundering and terrorist financing.

Within the United States, interagency cooperation has helped to foster a framework for a more unified front in combating money laundering and terrorist financing. In 2005, the Money Laundering Threat Assessment (MLTA) was produced by cooperating institutions consisting of experts from numerous U.S. government agencies, bureaus, and offices. The MLTA is a report that assists policy makers and regulators in understanding the current state of money laundering. It also offers tips in order to assist financial institutions in combating money laundering and terrorist financing. Policy makers, regulators, and financial institutions are not the only group of people getting assistance in combating money laundering and terrorist financing. Examiners of compliance programs have also gotten the assistance needed to ensure a financial institution's AML program is running as it should be.

The Federal Financial Institutions Examination Council (FFIEC) released revisions to the *Bank Secrecy Act/Anti–Money Laundering Examination Manual*. This manual is used by examiners to ensure that their clients' AML compliance programs are working as they should and helps protect the financial institutions, their customers, and the stakeholders from fines and penalties. With clever criminals trying to outsmart current AML programs, additional revisions are expected to be made to the FFIEC examination manual to further assist examiners and protect clients.

Despite major advancements in the unification of policies globally and at home, major inconsistencies and vague laws cause reason for concern. According to the Patriot Act, the term *financial institution* applies to many different industry types. Despite the fact that everything from a money services business (MSB) to an insurance company is considered a financial institution, different rules and laws apply to each different industry within the blanket "financial institution" category. For example, all insurance companies subject to the AML regulations are not presently required to have customer identification programs like banks do, but they are required to obtain and retain identifying information from customers in certain situations. Not only does this segregate insurance companies from the "financial institution" category, but also the vagueness of the regulation could cause fines to insurance companies that find it too complex to follow. FinCen and other agencies have already shown they are not afraid to fine companies that have problems understanding and complying with the Bank Secrecy Act revised by the Patriot Act.

In order to assure compliance with regulations and laws, FinCen has united with other agencies; together, they have been handing out fines to numerous industries. For example, BankAtlantic and a Kentucky MSB were fined for not complying with the Bank Secrecy Act. Together, these fines totaled over $10 million. As a way of deflecting regulatory scrutiny, many financial institutions are participating in "defensive filing." Defensive filing is when SARs are reported without the use of due diligence. This can dilute the data collection process for investigators and could allow important SARs to go unnoticed by FinCen. According to the latest SAR review, SAR filing increased 37 percent for depository institutions and 29 percent for MSBs from 2004 to 2005. Although defensive filing is causing a bit of problem, overall, the filing of SARs has helped combat money laundering and terrorist financing.

According to Issue 10 of the SAR report, numerous SARs were used to catch numerous criminals.For example, 15 SARs involved either indictments or arrests for alleged criminal behavior associated with the operation of an MSB involved in criminal activity; and 3 SARs filed involved the indictment of a corporation for acting as an unlicensed funds transmitter. This corporation had sent over $3.2 billion from shell companies to offshore accounts, and a single SAR detailed how a customer's pattern of money transfers mirrored that of an investment scheme. To ensure that all companies are complying with FinCen, numerous fines have been given to noncompliers.

In order to begin compliance with government standards, institutions, at the minimum, should apply the four pillars of the AML program. These four pillars are as follows:

1. Develop policies for preventing the institution from being used to launder money and dealing with cash and monetary instruments.
2. Designate a compliance officer to implement the anti-laundering program.
3. Establish a training program for all areas subject to laundering.
4. Establish an independent test/audit function that reviews and tests activities into specific accounts.

While these four pillars are a start, financial institutions should consider determining what best practices are accepted within their industries in order to ensure regulatory compliance and avoid fines or penalties.

Case Study: The Boys from Brazil

Business Challenge

A publicly traded U.S. company set up manufacturing operations in Brazil. Both the chief executive officer (CEO) and chief financial officer (CFO) of the operation were Brazilian nationals. There was no U.S. expatriate representation at the manufacturing plant.

The employees of the plant wanted to have half of their salary paid in U.S. dollars to avoid income tax, which was a common practice in the region. The local management decided to oblige the employees and set up an offshore bank account to make the cash payments.

Investigation

U.S. management became suspicious of the offshore account when the Brazilian management refused to provide details of the account. The investigation uncovered widespread fraud and abuse. The local management diverted millions from the business to the account. They used the money from this account to set up a competing manufacturing and retail operations managed by the wife of the CEO. The Brazilian management also paid themselves huge bonuses and paid for many personal expenses out of the account.

Results

The U.S. company paid huge fines and penalties for tax evasion and violation of anti–money laundering laws. The company was forced to close its Brazilian operation. The two Brazilian nationals maintained their competing business operations after the local police chief, who was also the father-in-law of the CEO, found no wrongdoing on their part.

CHAPTER 14

Procurement Fraud

Detecting and Preventing Procurement and Related Fraud

Bryan Moser and William P. Olsen

S ome have described procurement fraud as the least visible, yet most common and costly category of fraud among industries. In response, the federal government established the National Procurement Fraud Task Force on October 10, 2006, specifically dedicated to promote the prevention, early detection, and prosecution of procurement fraud. The principal focus of the task force includes several types of procurement and related fraud, such as:

- Kickbacks
- Vendor fraud
- Bid rigging
- Defective pricing
- Price fixing
- Contract fraud
- Cost/labor mischarging
- Product substitution
- Misuse of classified and sensitive information
- False claims
- Ethics and conflict of interest violations

While the task force was created from among government agencies, which are sensitive to risks to the government from procurement fraud, similar risks also exist across companies. Several of these types of procurement fraud are discussed in the sections that follow. Each section briefly defines the specific type of procurement fraud and discusses how one may consider investigating matters involving this type of fraud.

Kickbacks

Kickbacks are generally improper payments made to a company employee from an outside vendor. The end result is that one party gains an unfair advantage over another party through kickback payments or gifts. Relationships between employees and vendors frequently are hidden. Often, what appears to be an arm's-length business relationship is much more. Particular industries are susceptible to kickbacks, including, among others, medical and medical device, pharmaceutical, construction, defense contractors, construction, transportation, and precious metals.

To investigate these types of payments, expense accounts are reviewed for increased or suspicious activity, with specific attention being paid to the following types of accounts:

- Miscellaneous expense
- Commission expense
- Entertainment expense

As described by the Association of Certified Fraud Examiners (ACFE), a review of pertinent financial data is an appropriate task in any kickback investigation and should be done as early as possible. However, data often cannot be relied upon without question, as it may have been altered or falsified. Use of a certain amount of professional skepticism is important when reviewing records for outside third parties. One must ensure a sound basis for understanding:

- Who created the documents?
- Who controls the documents?
- How easy is it for these particular records to be altered, even in minor ways?
- How can I cross-reference what I find with other sources of information?

The Sniff Test

The fact that kickbacks can often be paid in the form of cash or goods makes them relatively more difficult to detect in books and records. The following scenarios should be investigated outside of the entity's documented business activity.

- *The vendor gift bearer.* Inappropriate gifts or lavish entertainment to an employee with purchasing authority.
- *The odd couple.* Your purchasing agent becomes the friend of an outside vendor.

- *The too-successful bidder.* A supplier who consistently wins without any apparent competitive advantage might be providing under-the-table incentives to obtain the work.

Other methods of detection include looking for price inflation, monitoring trends in cost of goods sold and services purchased (which may start small but increase over time), looking for excessive quantities purchased, investigating inventory shortages, looking for inferior goods purchased, background checks, net-worth analysis, and comparing actual to budgeted amounts.

According to the July 2004 article "Using the Law to Fight Fraud," published by the ACFE, "Regardless of the size of the company, the size of the vendor, or the company's rules and regulations that forbid such payments, kickbacks are paid frequently, depriving companies of much needed revenue, and often injuring the careers and reputations of the kickback recipient's co-workers."

Vendor Fraud

Vendor fraud is a term that spans a broad range of abuse—from fraudsters who create fictitious companies and submit bills for payment, to trusted suppliers who charge more than they are due. Vendors involved in fraudulent activity may even collude with your employees to help them navigate through your company's internal controls. To search for these instances of fraud, you could perform the following activities:

- Review vendor database for duplicate addresses.
- Compare employee database to vendor database for similar address and name.
- Identify vendor addresses that are mail drops.
- Perform extensive account reconciliation.
- Review journal entries (test a sample).
- Review invoices with missing purchase orders, duplicate or sequential invoice numbers by vendor, or duplicate date and amount.
- Look for ghost/shell vendors.
- Verify Social Security number.

Bid Rigging

The general definition of *bid rigging* is "competitors agree in advance that one bid of many will be the winning one on a contract that a public or private entity wants to let through competitive bidding." Bid rigging generally falls into one or more of the following general categories:

- *Bid suppression*. Agreeing to refrain from bidding.
- *Complementary bidding*. Agreeing to submit a similar but higher bid.
- *Bid rotation*. Agreeing to take turns at being bid winner.
- *Collusion*. Use of insider information to prepare and win the bid.

A number of patterns may indicate the potential of bid rigging. The U.S. Department of Justice (DOJ) lists the following situations as examples of such patterns:

- The same company always wins a particular procurement. This may be more suspicious if one or more companies continually submit unsuccessful bids.
- The same suppliers submit bids, and each company seems to take a turn being the successful bidder.
- Some bids are much higher than published price lists, previous bids by the same firms, or engineering cost estimates.
- Fewer than the normal number of competitors submit bids.
- A company appears to be bidding substantially higher on some bids than on other bids, with no apparent cost differences to account for the disparity.
- Bid prices drop whenever a new or infrequent bidder submits a bid.
- A successful bidder subcontracts work to competitors who submitted unsuccessful bids on the same project.
- A company withdraws its successful bid and subsequently is subcontracted work by the new winning contractor.

Since many parties can be involved in this type of fraud, often it can be cumbersome to investigate and perform a review of a significant amount of documentation. Methods commonly used to identify bid rigging entail conducting sample reviews of bid support; performing significant analysis of variances and relationships, such as manufacturing variances; ensuring that qualified individuals review the bids; understanding how the bids are rated, reviewed, and chosen; and determining if a particular vendor(s) is consistently selected.

Defective Pricing and Price Fixing

Defective pricing occurs when a contractor does not submit or disclose cost or pricing data that is accurate, complete, and current prior to reaching a price agreement. It can also take place when a provider is charging the victim a higher price than the agreed-upon price or is falsely representing prices in order to deceive the victim. This type of fraud may manifest itself on a gradual basis. This can occur after a contract is set in place if company employees are not attentive and the perpetrator begins to realize that company employees may not be attentive to the invoice approval process. The fraud may begin with small, infrequent amounts but may increase over time in size and frequency.

Price fixing is an agreement among competitors to raise, fix, or otherwise maintain the price at which their products or services are sold. These types of schemes can involve activities such as adhering to or setting a uniform price between competitors, eliminating discounts to the customer, keeping prices artificially high, establishing a minimum/floor pricing, agreeing to raise prices by a certain increment, changing prices without prior notification to other competitors, or fixing credit terms.

Identical prices at multiple entities may be a strong indicator of price fixing, but one must consider the broader economic environment in understanding the situation. The DOJ describes the following as situations that may be especially indicative of price fixing:

- Prices stay identical for long periods of time.
- Prices previously were different.
- Price increases do not appear to be supported by increased costs.
- Discounts are eliminated, especially in a market where discounts historically were given.
- Vendors are charging higher prices to local customers than to distant customers. This may indicate that local prices are fixed.

To detect and prevent these types of schemes, one could take actions such as:

- Test transactions for circumvention of controls or safeguards by activity such as manual overrides.
- Ensure separation of power in the approval and payment processing of invoices.
- Perform market research to compare prices with industry standards.
- Perform selected background checks to identify personal relationships between employees negotiating contracts and vendors.

Both bid rigging and price fixing can involve collusion among multiple competitors. While the nature of the fraud involves secrecy among the parties involved, certain patterns may be evident that would indicate such activity is more likely. The DOJ lists the following situations that may indicate collusion:

- The proposals or bid forms submitted by different vendors contain similar irregularities (such as identical calculations or spelling errors) or similar handwriting, typeface, or stationery. This may indicate that the designated low bidder may have prepared some or all of the losing vendor's bid.
- Bid or price documents contain white-outs or other physical alterations indicating last-minute price changes.
- A company requests a bid package for itself and a competitor, or submits both its and another's bids.
- A company submits a bid when it is incapable of successfully performing the contract (likely a complimentary bid).
- A company brings multiple bids to a bid opening and submits its bid only after determining (or trying to determine) who else is bidding.
- A bidder or salesperson makes:
  - Any reference to industry-wide or association price schedules.
  - Any statement indicating advance (nonpublic) knowledge of competitors' pricing.
  - Statements to the effect that a particular customer or contract "belongs" to a certain vendor.
  - Statements that a bid was a "courtesy," "complimentary," "token," or "cover" bid.
  - Any statement indicating that vendors have discussed prices among themselves or have reached an understanding about prices.

While specific steps were described earlier that may be employed to detect bid rigging or price fixing, the consideration of the presence of situations described immediately above can provide a broader context that more effectively focuses the investigative techniques for each individual situation.

Contract Fraud

Contract fraud is commonly associated with government contracts. The federal government has created strict guidelines related to disclosure of discounts and prices to nongovernmental commercial customers. However, contract fraud can also encompass various scenarios of fictitious acts occurring within both private and publicly held companies. Circumstances such as contracts written to limit competition (e.g., sole-source contracts), contracts awarded to the same vendor, who repeatedly wins on price by small margins, or contracts often being awarded to the last bid received are common signs of contract fraud. Following are some specific scenarios that can be indicators of contract fraud:

- *No-bid contracts.* Contracts awarded to related entities, friends, or relatives, often at a premium. Avoidance of the bidding process facilitates awarding a contract at above market rates or to a party that would otherwise not be considered most qualified for the project.
- *Excessive salaries.* A fraudster may take advantage of a situation where a contract budget contemplates two people performing separate functions. Instead of keeping the primary functions separate, the perpetrator may view the total salary for the two positions in aggregate and arrange to receive a much higher salary relative to another staff enlisted on the project. The perpetrator then delegates responsibilities to the other, less experienced staff. Thus, the expected benefit of two more senior resources is not realized by the contract.
- *Non-interest-bearing loans.* These loans generally are issued to senior staff members but without the knowledge of board members or other staff. Payment terms often are not delineated, and eligibility criteria are not determined. The potential for abuse is high in such instances.
- *Nepotism.* Unqualified relatives or friends are hired at above market rates or at rates that do not correspond to expertise or education level.
- *Related-party transactions.* Less-than-arm's-length transactions at above market rates that neither the board nor staff knows about.
- *Equipment retention.* Entity will purchase equipment and then create a lease contract in which the governmental organization makes the lease payments to the grant recipient. At the termination of the contract, the organization retains the right to the piece of equipment. Normally, equipment purchased with grant funds reverts back to the governmental organization. However, by claiming the equipment is leased, the grant recipient keeps the equipment at the termination of the contract.

You can identify red flags of potential exposure areas by reviewing the contract, cost reports, original budget, and relationships with subcontractors. ***The review should occur before the work begins!*** Although the original contract may have been reviewed for potential red flags, unusual items may surface during the performance of the contract that warrant follow-up.

Specific Questions to Ask Before

1. What type of contract is it?
2. Are equipment, maintenance, parts, and/or other specific inventory integral to the project?

3. Who approved company vendors and subcontractors?
4. Who are the key personnel, and who is responsible for approving invoices and reviewing cost reports?

Specific Questions to Ask After

1. Do invoices exist for materials with no "ship to" address indicated?
2. Do unusual items or purchases exist, such as materials or services that do not relate to the project?
3. Are there significant cost overruns that violate the terms of the contract?
4. Are there large budgets, or cost underruns, which may be used to transfer and conceal costs?
5. Are change orders excessive in relation to the original contract amount?
6. Are the same addresses or phone numbers listed among various vendor invoices?
7. Are there invoices with special processing notations such as "pay immediately"?
8. Are there hand-prepared invoices with vague, lacking, or general descriptions of the materials or services provided?
9. Are there purchases from unusual or nonpreferred vendors?
10. Is there a lack of inventory procedures or inadequate receiving procedures for valuable purchases?

Cost/Labor Mischarging

Schemes associated with cost/labor mischarging commonly involve contractors on cost-type contracts who fraudulently inflate the cost of labor or materials when invoicing customers and commonly charge for labor not performed or materials not used. It can also include misallocation of overhead costs to customers and overcharging of labor costs related to allocation of state and federal employment taxes (i.e., Federal Insurance Contributions Act [FICA], State Unemployment Tax Act of 2004 [SUTA], Federal Unemployment Tax Act [FUTA], etc).

Following are some potential indicia of fraud:

1. Rapidly increasing purchases from one vendor.
2. Rising expenses for goods and services with no related increase in production needs.
3. Excessive purchase of goods or services with no related increase in production needs.

In order to further identify this type of fraud, it is necessary to obtain an understanding of the internal controls and policies and procedures over the accounts payable (A/P) process. Areas in which one should consider analyzing and performing sample testing include:

- Invoice payments pattern (by account).
- Invoice payment pattern within vendor IDs for payment dates that are out of the range.
- Trends in the days of the week corresponding with invoice/payment dates, including invoices/payments generated on weekends.
- Gaps in check numbers, categorized by size of break (number of missing checks).
- Potential anomalies in payment and invoice activity:
  - Payment amount greater than invoice amount.
  - Payment amount equal to invoice amount.
  - Lack of detail on invoice supporting amount billed.

Preventive Methods

The preceding discussion focused largely on describing types of fraud and how to investigate suspected inappropriate activity. The more cost-effective approach to addressing procurement fraud is to take proactive steps. Preventative actions can include steps similar to those one would take to establish or enhance internal controls and corporate compliance guidelines. Following are some specific steps that can be implemented to assist in detecting and preventing future occurrences of procurement and related fraud:

1. *Segregation of duties.* Is more than one person creating orders, receiving invoices, and making payments?
2. *Supervisory controls.* Is someone watching?
3. *Receiving controls.* Who is receiving the invoices, and who is receiving the goods?
4. *Authorization controls.* How many people sign the checks?
5. *Reconciliation controls.* How frequently are bank statements reconciled to books and records, and by whom? Are they independent of other payable functions?
6. *Recording controls.* Does a well-defined and logical documentation process exist?
7. *Communication and training for employees.* Does everyone know what they should be doing, or can a savvy employee take advantage of others around him or her?
8. *Defined reporting lines and investigative measures.* Do employees know the consequences of their actions and whom they answer to?
9. *Consistent policies.* Prevention can be aided through consistent policies and procedures across an organization, especially if the organization

procures goods from many suppliers in different industries and countries.

10. *"Don't hide behind it!!"* Prosecute employee fraud. Most companies are too embarrassed to take action for fear of bad publicity or damage to the company's image. However, procurement or contract fraud is probably the least visible and most costly.

Benefits of Being Proactive

The ACFE estimates that U.S. companies lose as much as 7 percent of annual revenues to fraud. Studies also show that companies receive a 7-to-1 return on preventative and detective antifraud programs. Of course, it is not possible to know precisely how much any one company loses per year to fraud or how much fraud is prevented as a result of implementing prevention and detection programs. However, the aggregate risk of fraud and potential rewards of prevention could be large relative to the cost of implementing prevention and detection programs. Risks can be mitigated by performing a number of tangible steps.

Procurement fraud can involve companies large and small, domestic and international. Getting to the bottom of the situation can require highly specialized investigative skills, especially in very high-profile situations. Following are some example situations.

Case Study 1: Employee Fraud

Business Challenge

A privately held health care corporation suspected an employee of embezzling money through a fictitious vendor scheme. The company was not certain of the source of theft, but suspected possible theft due to evidence of the employee living beyond his salary.

Investigation Approach

In performing the investigation, the investigator searched for vendor fraud by comparing the percentage of expenditures represented by the 10 highest-volume vendors of the company over the past three years. As a result, a vendor was identified that had not appeared in prior years. An investigation of the nature of this relationship revealed a link between the vendor and the suspected employee. Interviews of current and former employees, as well as detailed computer forensic and data mining analysis, yielded significant information, resulting in the identification of $1.4 million dollars in fraudulent payments to the suspected employee.

Result

The company quickly terminated the employee and negotiated a plea bargain requiring the employee to identify any other employees involved in this scheme or other fraudulent activity. As part of the investigation, controls gaps were identified within the procurement process and remediation controls were provided to prevent and detect similar fraudulent activity. As mentioned earlier, the most cost-effective means to address procurement fraud is to implement steps to prevent such activity from occurring in the first place.

Case Study 2: Vendor Kickbacks and Collusion

Business Challenge

A large entity's former chief executive officer (CEO) was accused of taking vendor kickbacks and possible collusion. He was suing the company for a hefty sum for wrongful termination.

Investigation Approach

Through extensive interviews and computer forensic analysis, it was determined that the CEO executed contracts and/or business arrangements on behalf of the entity that either were not at arm's length or were not for the company's benefit. In addition, the CEO was receiving commission payments from the entity as compensation for providing the contracts and/or business arrangements. Indicia were also found that the CEO engaged in other businesses and had financial interests in other organization(s) that may have violated his employment agreement.

Result

The company was awarded $1 million in compensatory damages and $1.3 million in punitive damages for the counterclaim that was brought against the former CEO.

Conclusion

Procurement and related fraud can take several forms and can be a risk across many different organizations. Preventative measures can help minimize or avoid the consequences of these types of fraud. The specific steps to implement within any organization should be determined by those who have sufficient insight into the organization. That insight is best derived based on a comprehensive analysis of the organization and its risks and controls. This analysis may involve internal employees or external consultants or some combination.

CHAPTER 15

Construction Fraud

Monitoring, Mitigating, and Investigating Construction Fraud

James Schmid

All industry suffers from the cost of fraud. According to the Association of Certified Fraud Examiners' (ACFE's) *Report to the Nation on Occupational Fraud & Abuse (2008),* 7 percent of all business revenue is lost to fraud. Several other surveys of fraud indicate that the problem of fraud in the construction industry is significantly worse in severity than the average business. Fraud in the construction industry can be categorized into three basic types:

- Asset misappropriation
- Corruption
- Fraudulent financial statements

Frauds can involve a broad variety of schemes, irregularities, and illegal acts involving intentional deception. Notwithstanding this diversity, professionals involved in fighting fraud agree that every fraud usually has the following basic elements: a representation about a material fact that is false and made intentionally, knowingly, or recklessly, which is believed and acted upon by the victim, to the victim's damage.

As previously stated, there are three factors that generally underlie each fraud committed: (1) opportunity, (2) pressure, and (3) rationalization. These factors are referred to as the *fraud triangle:*

1. Opportunity is most often provided by weaknesses in the construction company's internal control systems such as:
   - Lack of proper separation of duties.

- Poor supervision and review.
- Poor contract and job site controls.
- Noncompliance with required procedure and project controls.
2. Pressure generally emanates from the employee's personal life or from upper management, for example:
    - Personal financial problems.
    - Poor lifestyle choices such as gambling, drugs, alcohol, or excessive debt.
    - Unrealistic deadlines or performance requirements from management.
    - Bonus or stock option plans tied to unrealistic performance criteria.
3. Rationalization is what a fraudster develops to justify his/her actions to himself/herself and authorities, for example:
    - "I will repay this money once my personal finances are in order."
    - "The company does not pay me what I am worth."
    - "Nobody will miss this money," or "this theft is victimless."
    - "The bosses are stealing from the customers; why shouldn't I steal from the bosses?"

Common Construction Company Fraud Schemes

According to the *2004 ACFE Report to the Nation on Occupational Fraud & Abuse,* the most common fraud in construction companies involves check tampering. Payroll fraud and skimming each occur about half as frequently as check tampering and the other common types of fraud, such as payroll, billing, corruption, fraudulent financial statements, and expense reimbursement fraud are the least frequent. However, some construction industry frauds can cost the construction company significantly more than the actual theft, due to the penalties and sanctions available under such laws as the False Claims Act or the Federal Acquisition Regulations (FARs) and/or due to diminished market reputation. Consequently, the prudent construction company will endeavor to protect itself against all types of fraud.

The following list provides a sample of the most common fraud schemes typically found in the construction industry:

1. *Asset misappropriation.* The theft of company assets or misuse of assets through fraudulent disbursements, skimming, or theft of cash or assets.
    - Fraudulent disbursements involve deceiving the construction company into disbursing funds without receiving a corresponding benefit such as goods or services. These schemes include:
        - Check tampering schemes involving altered or forged checks.
        - Billing schemes such as false invoices, altered invoices, shell companies, or false units on unit price contracts.

- Charging costs from lump-sum scope of work to a time-and-material change order.
- Modifying a subcontractor's scope of work or material specifications without issuing a deductive change order in return for payment in cash or as part of a barter transaction.
- Payroll schemes that use phantom employees, false labor hours, inappropriate wage rates, or diversion of funds intended for withholding accounts.
- Expense reimbursement schemes using false expense reporting or claiming illegitimate expenses.
- Skimming usually involves theft of cash or assets from the contractor before they have been recorded on the books. These schemes include:
  - Use of contractor assets or labor to do work for noncustomers in return for payment in cash or as part of a barter transaction.
  - Lapping sales receipts to cover up theft of sales revenue.
  - Writing off a legitimate receivable and diverting the funds actually received.
  - Creating a false refund and diverting the amount to a personal account.
  - Diversion of normal supplier refunds or rebates such as insurance or bond rebates.
- Theft of cash or assets from the contractor after it has been recorded on the contactor's books:
  - Theft of petty cash or cash on hand.
  - Theft of bank deposits.
  - Purchasing fungible materials and diverting a portion for personal gain.

2. *Corruption.* The use of inappropriate influence in a business transaction in order to establish undue advantage over an organization and/or the other parties competing to participate in the transaction.
   - Bribes, bid rigging, and the leaking of confidential information during the bidding process.
   - Bribes and kickbacks received for contract selection, approval of change order pricing, schedule modification, material substitution, or favorable site/sequence access.
   - Market division or market sharing among competitors.
   - Conflicts of interest.
   - Employment of illegal (undocumented) workers.
   - Fraudulent reporting of safety, minority content, environmental, or other information required by a construction contract or by a government regulatory entity.

3. *Fraudulent financial statements.* The willful and material falsification of the construction company's financial statements. The two primary areas

of greatest risk for financial statement fraud are revenue recognition and the concealment of liabilities. Specific examples of financial statement fraud include:

- Overstating revenues by overstating the percent complete of construction projects in process.
- Accounting for construction claims and disputes as change orders and recognizing the revenue inappropriately.
- Moving cost overruns from completed projects to new projects to avoid recognizing a loss in the current period.
- Overstating the value of assets.
- Capitalizing expenses as assets.
- Rounding up transactions intended to inflate revenue or to divert costs to a subsequent period.

Combating Fraud and Corruption

Of the three elements of the fraud triangle (opportunity, pressure, and rationalization), the element of opportunity is most easily within the control of the construction company. The opportunity to commit a fraud can be lessened in a number of ways, the most effective of which are:

- Strong internal controls.
- Comprehensive compliance and ethics program—we cover compliance in Chapter 9.
- Embraced and demonstrated by top management.
- An appropriate system for reporting potential problems.
- Timely follow-up of identified noncompliance and appropriate discipline.
- Internal audit.
- Proper vetting of employees and business partners.

Strengthen Your Internal Controls

The most frequent shortcoming underlying fraud in a construction company is poor internal controls. Following are some of the most effective and often overlooked internal controls a construction company should implement and routinely monitor:

- New-hire background checks.
- Separation of responsibilities, particularly in the accounting department and particularly:

- Entering accounting data.
- Writing checks.
- Signing checks.
- Reviewing supporting data and documents to confirm that expenses are appropriate and properly classified.
- Bank reconciliations.
- Bank statements (and other mail) should be opened and filed by someone other than the person writing checks.
- There should be no more than three manual checks per month.
- Bank reconciliations should be reviewed by management.
- Process disbursements in a systematic way.
- Check runs should be processed once a week.
- There should be only one check register per bank account.
- Code purchase orders, work orders, and invoices.
- Establish and follow a document and data retention policy.
- Conduct routine computer backup procedures.
- Obtain supplier and subcontractor confirmations.
- Establish and follow routine bid procedures for subcontracts and major suppliers, and maintain bid files with:
  - Bid packages.
  - Bids received.
  - Bid evaluations.
- Invoice construction project owners using standard G702 and G703 forms and randomly:
  - Test math on both forms.
  - Test line-item support documentation.
  - Test the roll-forward of data from one month to the next.
- Set up unique job cost reports and bank accounts for each major construction project.
- Tie the schedule of values to the contract plus change orders.
- Avoid mixing time and material and lump-sum work.
- Securely maintain all project insurance certificates and all contracts.
- Randomly confirm that insurance certificates are accurate.
- Require that all material delivered to the site be received and that the shipping documents are secured and provided to accounting.
- Pay invoices only after matching them to the purchase order and the receiving documentation.
- Do no work without a signed contract, change order, or work order.
- Require the applications for payment to tie to the job cost report.
- The schedule of values should be maintained and measured against actual.

CHAPTER **16**

Special Investigations
How to Investigate Allegations of Corruption
Dorsey Baskin and William P. Olsen

C orporate scandals sometimes seem as ubiquitous as TV crime dramas. Recent events in the business world illustrate the sweeping impact fraud and other illegal activities have on organizations, investors, and stakeholders. When an organization's board receives an alert about potential wrong-doing, it must evaluate the credibility of the alert, respond appropriately, and prevent further damage. To do so, organizations should understand the perspectives of the external auditor and forensic accountant on the special investigation process, as well as the roles of their boards of directors and other key players.

When an alert comes in regarding potential wrongdoing that is material, organizations should have a fraud/illegal act contingency plan in place that coordinates the needs of various parties, from general counsel and internal auditors to the chief executive officer and management. A solid contingency plan has a decision tree to ensure that proper steps are taken in the event of suspected fraud and other illegal acts. If fraud or other illegal acts are suspected, a company should take the following actions:

- Notify the audit committee and board of directors.
- Evaluate the need to engage an independent outside attorney.
- Inform the external auditor.
- Communicate as needed to employees to maximize document retention.
- Preserve potential evidence.
- Where applicable, safeguard the premises and property.
- Isolate continued risks.
- If appropriate, notify the insurance company.

- If appropriate, inform the proper authorities.
- Inform applicable state and federal regulatory agencies.
- Work with counsel to determine if communication should be made to the outside if the company is publicly traded.
- Where applicable, gather information from outside parties.

An Interested Party: The Auditor

Issues are generally considered to be more significant when they may implicate senior management, may materially affect past or future financial statements, or may involve violations of law and regulations. If a significant issue arises, the audit committee should communicate with the external auditor immediately. Periodic meetings are useful to evaluate the matter being investigated, any potential internal control or financial reporting implications, and the auditor's needs and expectations. Communication should remain open, thorough, and continuous during the investigation. The auditor will need to have access to the:

- Complaint/allegation.
- Investigation work plan and schedule.
- Interview plan and findings, if any.
- Interviewees.
- Documents used (including electronic documents).
- Investigation findings on violations of policy, law, and regulations.

There are a number of reasons why complete and open communication with the auditor is important and why an audit committee will want to make sure its investigation is objective and thorough. For example, if the investigating committee is considering using internal or regular corporate legal counsel to perform the investigation, the auditor should be given the opportunity early on to evaluate whether, given the severity of the allegations and/or the level in the organization of the subject individuals, he or she will be satisfied with that approach or whether external resources are necessary to provide sufficient objectivity.

Among other things, in order to complete an audit and rely on representations in and underlying the financial statements, the auditor needs to reach a conclusion regarding the integrity of management and the board of directors. An investigation of senior management or board members by regular internal or external corporate counsel may not bring either the appearance or actual objectivity needed, and the earlier this question is resolved, the less likely it is that the organization will incur costs for work that may need to be redone.

In addition, all potentially material disclosures and accounting implications must be evaluated. For Securities and Exchange Commission (SEC) registrant companies, the auditor must evaluate his or her responsibility under section 10A of the Exchange Act, which may require a direct report to the SEC detailing any likely illegal acts. The auditor's determination of the need to report directly to the SEC will depend on an evaluation of the adequacy of the investigation and remedial actions taken.

The auditor also must assess in a timely manner any financial statement restatement needs, for example, whether to withdraw prior audit reports, whether management needs to file a "no reliance" Form 8-K, and whether a previous auditor needs to be involved. To reach these conclusions, the auditor needs to be satisfied that the scope of the investigation will be adequate. Very often, the investigation is too narrowly focused on the known or alleged wrongdoings when the auditor's concern extends also to earlier periods and to any other acts the suspected person or persons may have committed.

In the case of fraud or other illegal activity, the root cause can lie in weak internal controls. The auditor must determine how the breakdown impacts the audit work plan and, ultimately, evaluate whether to continue the client relationship.

Although attorney-client privilege is generally a priority for the investigating committee, it may need to be waived for the sake of the auditor's need for information to complete his or her audit and comply with his or her professional responsibilities. When needed information is not forthcoming, audit reports can be delayed at the expense of compliance with loan covenants, regulatory filing deadlines, and other important company requirements.

All of these concerns force the auditor to pay attention to significant and potentially significant allegations of wrongdoing. Starting with the evaluation of the potential significance of the allegations, all the way through to the conclusion of the investigation and any remedial action, the auditor has a strong and necessary interest. If the auditor is not informed and consulted throughout the process, the auditor may not be satisfied with the investigation (resulting in delays and added cost), but unnecessary suspicion may be created as to why the auditor was not earlier informed and consulted.

Once the investigation wraps up, the auditor may want a special representation letter signed by the investigating board committee. The letter provides a written record of communications with the auditor, placing the committee on record as to, among other things, its conclusions about the adequacy and completeness of the investigation, the completeness of the auditor's access to the investigation granted by the committee, and the adequacy and completeness of any remedial action by the company.

The Special Investigation

If an attorney is hired to perform an investigation, often he or she will engage a forensic accountant for assistance in gathering, analyzing, and reporting on the subject of the investigation. The forensic accountant's work often involves several phases.

Phase One: Collecting Documents

When it comes to collecting documents, more is better. Once allegations or suspicions of fraud or other illegal or unethical activity have been raised, err on the side of caution when gathering documents to minimize the risk of destroyed or lost records. In today's world, it is often not enough to follow the paper trail. Electronic data usually is collected from the network, hard drives, and external sources like web sites. In addition, data can be mined from cell phone records, voice mails, video surveillance, and access systems.

Although it seems like electronic information can be erased with the simple click of a mouse, data often remains even if the file housing it has been removed. However, it takes special expertise to unearth these documents. Computer forensics specialists can help recover, secure, and reconstruct data that otherwise may be missing, incomplete, or unusable. They can also safely and securely house the data in organized and searchable interfaces.

Phase Two: Searching Public Records

Public record searches provide another piece of the puzzle and can help develop a profile of the target individual or organization. In addition, public record searches can identify previous criminal or unethical activity and identify where misappropriated assets were hidden.

Phase Three: Interviewing Employees and Suspects

The interview process is more than just a Q&A session. It begins with careful and deliberate planning. Interviewers must do their homework and know the facts, including the background of the interviewee, before a face-to-face session takes place. The interviewer must also sequence the questions and the interviews properly.

It is always appropriate and necessary to have a witness present during an interview to assure that key information from the interview is captured and documented properly.

Phase Four: Examination and Analysis

In the examination and analysis phase of an investigation, the investigator processes, sorts, dissects, and starts to draw conclusions from the data gathered during the first three phases. The goal is to determine how long the activity has gone on, the financial impact of the activity, who knew about the wrongdoing and what they did once they became aware of it. As evidence is gathered, it is also necessary to evaluate continuously the scope of the investigation and whether other persons and activities need to be examined.

A large portion of analysis boils down to following the money. The investigator may identify suspicious activity, such as wire transfers to known money laundering havens or payments being made through shell companies or agents. Finally, a significant focus will be placed on analyzing correspondence of involved parties, especially e-mails, and performing data-mining techniques on the organization's electronic data that signal any red flags.

Prevention Is Key

No organization is immune from fraud and other illegal acts; however, safeguards can be put in place to help deter it. The tone from the top is integral. A code of ethical conduct that is tied to corporate values is the first line of defense. Whistle-blowers also need a safe way to report suspicious activity, and management must respond appropriately. Build a strong internal control system and regularly evaluate it. Turn the magnifying glass on your organization's culture and controls to deter wrongdoing before it occurs.

Navigating the Perils of the Global Marketplace

William P. Olsen, R. Kirt West, Nancy R. Grunberg, and Danette R. Edwards

During the past several years, the Foreign Corrupt Practices Act of 1977 (FCPA) has enjoyed an unprecedented renaissance, as the U.S. Securities and Exchange Commission (SEC) and the U.S. Department of Justice (DOJ) have increasingly turned to it to penalize domestic and overseas companies, as well as individuals, suspected of bribing foreign officials to secure business.Congress initially passed the FCPA in 1977 in the wake of the Watergate scandal and after discovering that more than 400 corporations had made questionable or illegal payments to foreign officials to gain business or smooth business processes. The FCPA aims to prevent bribery of foreign officials and encourage the establishment of certain accounting controls and practices. The FCPA applies to companies whose securities are registered with the SEC, and certain of its provisions extend duties and liabilities to registered companies based on the conduct of their partly owned subsidiaries. This chapter is concerned with *both* the bribery and accounting provisions of the FCPA and the special compliance and enforcement challenges that each present in certain regions of the world.

FCPA Enforcement

The year 2007 was a watershed period for FCPA enforcement: The DOJ instituted 16 FCPA prosecutions in 2007, as compared to 4 only five years before. A special FCPA task force within the Federal Bureau of Investigation (FBI) was also established in 2007. In announcing the task force, the FBI's assistant director, Chip Burrus, proclaimed that the agency's "highest criminal priority is to curb public corruption, whether here or overseas. . . ." The SEC has filed more than 30 FCPA actions within the past two years. In 2008, the rate of filing of FCPA enforcement actions outpaced that of 2007. All signs indicate that this trend will continue. In the future, enforcement may even be fueled by a limited class of private litigants, as outlined in a recent proposal to amend the act.

The recent spike in FCPA enforcement is undoubtedly the result of companies moving more aggressively into "emerging markets" where anti-bribery laws tend to be somewhat lax and bribes are often viewed as a normal part of the business process. Indeed, a large number of 2007 and 2008 cases involved emerging markets. As was discussed earlier, often, poorly trained employees in these environments assume a "when in Rome" attitude, not realizing that the local way of doing business may be a direct violation of U.S. laws and regulations. Many companies that fail to evaluate the full landscape of risks before entering a new market later find themselves faced with an investigation centering on potential FCPA violations.

Managing FCPA investigations in emerging markets can be even more complex than transnational investigations in established markets, and companies need to understand these complexities in order to avoid the creation of additional liabilities. The remainder of this chapter presents a high-level overview of issues arising in FCPA investigations in emerging markets, along with practical tips for preventing and dealing with these issues.

When gathering facts in situations other than responding to a government inquiry, companies have some flexibility in how to characterize those activities at the site of the foreign operation. Depending on the characterization (compliance monitoring vs. auditing vs. investigation), a company may encounter different levels of resistance in the foreign environment. For instance, a 2008 DOJ Advisory Opinion details the difficulties that a major U.S. company and its wholly owned foreign subsidiary experienced when attempting to conduct due diligence on a foreign private company owner who would be considered a "foreign official" under the FCPA. The due diligence was undertaken in order to alleviate FCPA concerns related to a series of intended transactions whereby both the subsidiary and the foreign private company owner would acquire an entity responsible for managing certain public services for a foreign municipality. The foreign owner refused to make or accede any disclosures regarding his various roles or corporate interests, asserting, "In the foreign country it was neither necessary nor customary to do so." Ultimately, the U.S. company was forced to approach various high-ranking government officials who confirmed some of its concerns. While the Opinion does not reveal the country in which this took place, it appears to have occurred in a socialist, state-run economy, where many of these fact-finding concerns arise.

In some jurisdictions, it may be easier to obtain official approvals to conduct auditing or compliance monitoring than to perform an investigation. How a company refers to fact-gathering activities at the foreign site may rest partly on who is performing those activities (lawyers vs. nonlawyer professionals, including forensic auditors, computer forensic specialists, and investigators). As with many other issues, it is advisable to obtain the advice of local counsel at the outset of the project.

The involvement of nonlawyer professionals in foreign countries raises an important issue: To what extent, if at all, would a U.S. court apply the attorney-client privilege to communications involving these professionals overseas? In all probability, the answer to this question will turn on the law of the country with the greatest nexus to the subject of the inquiry.

U.S. courts have shown a willingness to apply privilege protection to communications with a nonlawyer in a foreign country where the nonlawyer is, consistent with foreign custom, essentially acting as an attorney in connection with the subject matter of the communication. Privilege concerns are not limited to situations involving nonlawyers. In emerging markets, communications with in-house lawyers in the course of FCPA monitoring, audits, and investigations may not qualify for privilege protection. This issue underscores the need for consulting local counsel concerning applicable privileges in the foreign jurisdiction. It also may argue for the use of practitioners from the U.S. because of the strong protection American courts give to attorney-client communications and work product.

There are also operational hurdles to gathering facts abroad. Immigration regulations in emerging markets may require outside counsel and nonlawyer professionals (depending on their country of origin) to obtain business visas. Where business visas are needed, outside counsel must understand any work restrictions imposed. For instance, some countries prohibit business travelers from conducting interviews, writing reports, and carrying out computer forensics. The good news for defense counsel is that similar work restrictions apply to government lawyers and other officials traveling abroad on "judicially related official business." Such business includes activities such as interviewing witnesses, taking depositions, or conducting investigations and inspections. Government officials must secure permission from the host country to conduct these activities; this requirement usually means that a diplomatic note must be sent to the Ministry of Foreign Affairs requesting permission. (See U.S. Attorneys Manual 3-8.730, for example.)

Once a company has made early decisions regarding the use of outside lawyers and nonlawyer professionals and ironed out the broad operational issues, it can concentrate on the mechanics of fact-gathering activities. To a large degree, this task means determining how to conduct an appropriate records review. This portion of an investigation can be quite challenging for many companies, even when there are only domestic concerns involved, especially when it comes to the preservation and processing of electronic records. The process can be fraught with additional difficulties in emerging markets resulting from the different laws, languages, and attitudes toward record keeping in those jurisdictions.

Record Keeping

As an example of the difficulty that may be encountered in emerging market countries, record-keeping practices in Asia differ widely from those in the United States. In China, official tax receipts are known as *fa piao*. These documents are official receipts received by the purchaser of goods and services from establishments. They are used by establishments to document the sale of goods and services for tax purposes as part of China's Value Added Taxation (VAT) system. Companies in China must maintain these documents as proof of the business expenses for which employees are reimbursed, such as meals or lodging. The *fa piao*, however, show only the amount and the company "chop" (official company stamp) of the establishment that issues them; they do not show details of the transaction, such as the nature of the goods or services provided.

This system does not provide for the transparency of transactions that is commonplace in the United States and presents a stark contrast to the American approach to record keeping. After Congress expanded the federal obstruction of justice laws in 2002 via the Sarbanes-Oxley Act, many companies invested substantial resources in the design (or redesign) and implementation of robust corporate records and information management programs for their U.S. offices. The December 2006 e-discovery amendments to the Federal Rules of Civil Procedure prompted many companies to redouble their records management efforts over the years following, at least with respect to U.S. operations.

In light of the recent spate of FCPA cases charging books and records violations, companies would be well advised to focus their attention on record-keeping practices abroad. The accounting provisions of the FCPA contain both internal controls requirements and record-keeping requirements. Broadly speaking, the internal controls provisions require companies to establish a framework of internal controls that will ensure that transactions are appropriately authorized and that transactions are recorded as necessary to permit preparation of financial statements in accordance with generally accepted accounting principles or other applicable laws. The record-keeping provisions require companies to maintain accurate books and records that "in reasonable detail accurately and fairly reflect the transactions and disposition of the [company's] assets."

Failure to abide by the FCPA's accounting provisions can expose companies and individuals to significant fines and penalties. Some well-publicized recent fines in cases involving allegations of FCPA accounting violations exceeded $30 million and $40 million. The threat of these stiff penalties, coupled with the known risks of inadequate record-keeping practices in certain emerging-market countries, make overseas records management initiatives a corporate governance imperative that guarantees to smooth the process of data collection in an investigation.

Data Collection and Processing

One of the many challenges in conducting an investigation abroad is ensuring that information obtained on targeted individuals, whether the information consists of hard-copy records or electronic data recovered by computer forensic techniques, actually pertains to the targeted person. For instance, in China there often are problems in translating the individual's English name into Chinese because of the many characters found in the Chinese language. People are commonly mistaken for others. In addition, the commonality of last names in China can make it exceedingly difficult to be confident that any information retrieved about an individual is in fact referring to that individual and not another individual with the same name. In Latin American countries, the convention of having the mother's maiden name at the end of an individual's surname can potentially lead to the misidentification of individuals.

With respect to financial records, as evidenced by the *fa piao* in China, the accounting records that must be maintained in emerging markets may be very different, in both content and format, from those that are maintained in the United States and the European Union. Often, records are not in electronic form and may be extremely difficult to retrieve.

For these reasons, it may be desirable to have the assistance of an independent local forensic accounting firm that can provide cultural and language assistance during an investigation. The local forensic accounting firm will know what records are available, will know where such records can be found, and, of course, can provide invaluable assistance in reviewing such records. Similarly, these same language skills will be critical in conducting an effective forensic search of computers and servers and analyzing records discovered during the search.

Transborder Data-Flow Issues

Pitfalls and hurdles for U.S. lawyers in gathering facts abroad are not only limited to emerging markets. For example, the European Union's directive on data privacy has been in place since 1995. The EU directive served as a model for the personal data protection laws of Argentina and Poland, to name a few examples, and other emerging market countries may look to it if and when they adopt or amend their own data protection laws. It creates some hurdles to the gathering and use of information, such as that contained in e-mails. In brief, the EU directive and the laws of Argentina and Poland essentially require consent to use personal data and place limits on the transmission of personal data to third-party countries. Even within-company transfers are not allowed if the recipient jurisdiction does not have adequate data protection laws of its own. Violations of the transfer rules are punishable through fines, penalties, lawsuits, and other sanctions. EU member states have implemented the strictures of the EU directive through their own data protection legislation. Some EU member states already had substantial privacy protection regimes in place well before the EU directive took effect, and the EU directive was a mere supplement. Additionally, some countries' privacy laws contain criminal blocking statutes that criminalize the export of specific categories of documents and information. Also, depending on the country, banks may be restricted from disclosing certain data pursuant to bank secrecy laws. In the future, these more stringent rules could also find a place in the privacy protection laws of emerging market countries.

Accordingly, before reviewing and/or exporting documents or data in an international FCPA investigation, counsel must be aware of the nuances in the privacy and data protection laws of the applicable countries. Finally, it is important for companies and defense counsel to realize the value of data protection laws, blocking statutes, and bank secrecy laws as bases for potential objections to evidence gathering (and sharing) by governmental authorities in international investigations.

Government enforcement authorities in post-9/11 society appear more committed than ever to information sharing. There are a handful of mechanisms available to governmental authorities for evidence-gathering (and -sharing) purposes in international investigations. Mutual Legal Assistance in Criminal Matters Treaties (MLATs) are a prime example. MLATs are treaties between the United States and other nations that govern cooperation between the DOJ and other foreign prosecuting authorities. Through MLATs, other countries provide the DOJ with evidence from foreign companies and individuals for use in U.S. investigations and proceedings, and vice versa. MLATs also generally allow criminal authorities to share requested information with regulatory agencies (e.g., the SEC or its foreign counterparts, such as the Hong Kong Securities and Futures Commission), and to request information for the purpose of assisting regulatory investigations. MLATs generally allow witnesses to be summoned, documents and other evidence to be produced, searches to be executed, and process to be served. The United States has numerous MLATs in force, including ones with the following countries with emerging markets: Argentina, Brazil, Hong Kong SAR, India, Korea, Mexico, Poland, the Russian Federation, South Africa, and Turkey.

In addition to MLATs, governmental authorities can obtain information through less formal, case-by-case arrangements between the regulatory bodies of different nations. In this regard, the SEC often utilizes what are known as memoranda of understanding, or MOUs, which provide for the sharing of evidence and cooperation in compliance and enforcement efforts. MOUs can be used to collect evidence for civil and criminal investigations. The SEC's arrangements with other countries also include frameworks for cooperation and less specific exchanges. Another method whereby the SEC gathers evidence is issuance of domestic subpoenas for the production of data located in a foreign country.

For companies, the existence of each of these data-collection and— sharing methods means that evidence located abroad might become available to the U.S. government (or, conversely, to a foreign government) if a government investigation is initiated outside of the United States. Once foreign documents are accessible to one nation's governmental authorities, other governments can potentially gain access to them through MLATs, MOUs, or other similar treaties or agreements. The risk of incurring additional liabilities in multiple legal systems as a result of international information-sharing policies should be taken into consideration in deciding whether to voluntarily cooperate with certain government agencies in matters implicating the FCPA or foreign bribery laws.

The risk of incurring multiple types of liabilities as a result of providing information to one governmental authority and then having that information shared with other authorities is not limited to cooperation between sovereign nations. Domestic parallel proceedings by the DOJ and SEC in cases involving FCPA violations are typical, with the SEC sometimes tacking on additional securities fraud claims. In light of this phenomenon, defense counsel and companies must carefully weigh the decision to cooperate in a civil FCPA investigation, as it could lead to criminal liability in a domestic parallel proceeding.

The DOJ and the SEC have substantially increased their focus on the FCPA in the past several years and regard the FCPA as their most potent weapon in combating foreign corruption. With this increased focus on the FCPA, the overseas operations of U.S.-based corporations will be facing more scrutiny. U.S. corporations that proactively investigate potential FCPA violations and self-report the findings to the DOJ and the SEC are less likely to face some of the harsher penalties that can be imposed by these agencies. Understanding the unique challenges in conducting FCPA investigations in emerging-market countries will help counsel provide effective representation for the client and reduce the risk to the client.

CHAPTER 18

Case for Collective Action[1]

The World Bank Initiative

William P. Olsen, Djordjija Petrowski, and Sterl Greenhalgh

I had the pleasure of working with the World Bank Institute on an initiative called "Fighting Corruption: The Case for Collective Action." The institute brought together a group that represented industry, public accounting, not-for-profit organizations, and representatives from the World Bank to brainstorm ways to work together to address the issue of global corruption. The result was a manual on collective action, which lays out ways that organizations can work with governments, industries, and the public to try to level the playing field in the global marketplace. The group was represented by organizations such as Grant Thornton LLP, United Nations Compact, Center for International Private Enterprise (CIPE), Transparency International, Global Advice Network, and Siemens. The results of this initiative are included in this chapter.

Why Collective Action against Corruption?

Corruption is a crucial problem for all—companies, governments, and citizens alike. Over the past decade, the amount of attention devoted to corruption has grown exponentially. Yet, while we increasingly talk about the problem and recognize that it must be dealt with, the need for effective anti-corruption tools remains pressing.

One such tool is collective action. The idea is simple: Get companies working together with their competitors and other stakeholders to create

---

[1]Reprinted with permission, © The World Bank Group, All Rights Reserved.

markets where decisions are driven by economic considerations and not by corrupt transactions. Implementing this idea, however, is more difficult. How do we convince companies that it is in their interest to work with their competitors to eliminate bribery? How do we convince them that it makes economic sense to invest their individual resources to reduce bribery? What are the key components of collective action against corruption? What is the business case for it? Where should companies begin?

These are all interesting questions that this chapter will attempt to answer. Before we get into collective action, however, it is useful to take a closer look at the different faces of corruption and how they affect the private sector. Similarly, we must look at the private sector not as a monolith, but as a complex web of companies with different priorities, resources, and perspectives. Doing so will help us set the groundwork for understanding what collective action is all about.

Different Views of Corruption

Short definition: Corruption is the misuse of entrusted power for personal or private gain.

While we can broadly define corruption as the misuse of entrusted power for personal or private gain, we must dig deeper, beyond the traditional definition to see that corruption is much more than bribery. In reality, corruption has many different faces, and recognizing which is which is absolutely crucial to effective anti-corruption programs.

From the private-sector perspective, corruption can be separated into several distinct areas, such as bribery, extortion, state capture, political financing, and others.

Particularly important is the difference between bribery and extortion. While in the case of bribery the private sector may be seen as a facilitator of a corrupt transaction, in the case of extortion, companies may actually fall victim to public officials with discretionary authority.

Also interesting is the state capture concept. The idea behind it is that companies may utilize the weak rule-of-law institutions to stifle competition and obtain favorable market positions. Such processes often are difficult to observe and capture, especially in developing countries where transparency is lacking.

Business Costs of Corruption

Corruption may appear to some business owners to be necessary for success, but actually it:

- Carries costly fines and penalties for companies.
- Results in costly fines, penalties, and jail terms for individuals.
- Results in loss of business reputation.

Costs of Corruption for Industries, Economies, and Countries

The traditional view of corruption suggests that it is good for business. Some have said, for example, that it is necessary to "grease the wheels of commerce." But is this really the case?

What we have seen around the world is that while corruption may benefit individual companies in the short term—for example, in gaining ground on competition in individual transactions—over time, it becomes a real barrier to development and business growth. It becomes a barrier to development on the company level, on the industry level, on the national economy level, and on the global level as well.

In other words, from the private-sector perspective, corruption is about costs.

Corruption is about personal costs; it can ruin careers and reputation and result in criminal, civil, or employment sanctions.

Corruption is about company-level costs; it increases costs of doing business, it undermines innovation, and it diverts investment elsewhere. For example, the World Bank estimates that costs of corruption have surpassed $1 trillion. A recent survey also highlights the costs of corruption for companies in terms of lost market opportunities or fines and penalties.

Corruption is about economic and social costs; it undermines the rule of law and keeps foreign investors at bay, preventing job creation and limiting sustainable development. Think about it this way: Transparency International estimates that former Indonesian leader Suharto embezzled anywhere from US$15 to $35 billion from his country, while Ferdinand Marcos in the Philippines, Mobutu in Zaire, and Abacha in Nigeria may have embezzled up to US$5 billion each. This is money that could have gone toward developing a sound economic base—providing a better life for whole sectors of society by creating jobs and generating wealth.

Different Views of the Private Sector

Different companies have different resources and interests.

Business—just like corruption—is not monolithic. It has many different faces. It is important to recognize the different forms of the private sector, because different companies wield different power in an economy and therefore are affected differently by corruption. For example, while a handful

of powerful business elites and cronies may monopolize access to government, smaller firms and informal entrepreneurs will have very different
interests.

Generally, it is useful to subdivide companies into the following sectors:

- National/multinational companies
- Small and medium-sized enterprises (SMEs)
- State-owned enterprises
- Informal-sector firms
- Leading-edge firms

There are, of course, others, but these categories capture more broadly
the different faces of business. Consider, for example, leading-edge firms
(those seeking to attract investment and to develop new technologies) on the
one hand and informal-sector firms on the other. They operate in different
markets and interact with different government agencies, and while they
may suffer from the overall problem of corruption, they will approach it
differently. It may be more difficult for an informal-sector company to stand
up to corruption, while a larger firm may be more concerned with putting
in place internal governance tools to detect and prevent bribery.

The bottom line: Different companies have different resources and interests, and the private sector should not be thought of as a monolith but rather
as a number of different firms.

Corruption Dilemma

The private sector can be a *source* of corruption; the private sector can be
a *victim* of corruption (see Figure 18.1).

As established previously, there is a variety of different companies
and many different forms of corruption. So here we get to the corruption
dilemma!

In some cases, as commonly recognized, the private sector can be a
source of corruption. One example is companies providing bribes to get
favorable transactions approved or trying to win tenders over competitors.
In other cases, however, the private sector can be a *victim* of corruption.
Increasingly, the negative impact of corruption that businesses face in their
normal operations is becoming recognized, although the understanding is
still not as widespread as with companies being a source of corruption.
For example, we are seeing in many developing countries that the costs of
corruption for SMEs and broader economic development are becoming a
key electoral issue.

FIGURE 18.1 Corruption Dilemma for Private Sector

How do we reconcile these two views—that the private sector can be both a victim and a source of corruption? We can look at corruption from yet another angle and declare that the private sector can in fact be a solution to the corruption problem. How is this possible?

Well, the private sector can do many things. Some solutions can come in the form of mobilizing the business community for reform. Some can come in the form of saying "no" to corruption. Companies also can seek to reform their internal institutions—this is where corporate governance comes into play.

Let's look at how the private sector can be a solution to corruption in more detail.

Private-Sector Institutes

There are two types of anti-corruption efforts for the private sector:

- Setting up internal mechanisms to prevent corruption.
- Reforming internal operating environment to reduce corruption opportunities.

Generally, private-sector solutions to corruption can be divided into two different categories.

On the one hand, companies may seek to reform internally, to reduce opportunities for corruption. This is where good corporate governance comes in as an effective anti-corruption tool. Not only does good governance within companies make bribes harder to give, it also makes them harder to conceal. Good governance can be effective in reducing corruption at all levels—both on the board level and on the staff level. It does so by making sure that anti-corruption policies are not just statements, but that they are actually implemented. Cleaning up internal company climate is important for other reasons as well—companies themselves must be transparent before they try to convince the government and the public broadly to stand up to corruption. A useful tool developed by Transparency International that can help companies put in place effective internal anti-corruption policies are the *Business Principles for Countering Bribery*.

On the other hand, companies may engage in efforts to reform the environment within which they operate. This relates to broader issues of institutional and business climate reform. This also includes efforts to mobilize the business community and work with competitors. Why would companies seek to do this? Because, simply put, more effective markets with transactions within a rule-of-law system present more opportunities for business growth and development. In other words, companies not only take advantage of markets, they also want to create new market opportunities. Consider public procurement projects in corruption-prone countries. Although companies may seek to make each individual transaction transparent, they may also engage in a broader effort to streamline procurement laws and create a climate where decisions are less susceptible to corruption.

What these different private-sector approaches to combating corruption mean is that there are different sources of corruption. In other words, since corruption is so complex and is caused by a variety of factors, no one approach alone will be successful in reducing it.

So what are these sources of corruption? The reality of doing business in developing countries is that opportunities for corruption often arise when companies explore ways to avoid inefficiency. In other words, corruption thrives in systems plagued by inadequate, unclear, excessive, unpublicized, and frequently changing laws and regulations. Similarly, such systems create incentives for companies to exploit inefficiencies, driving corruption as well.

In addition to weak legal and regulatory systems, sources of corruption include:

- Lack of transparency and accountability in the public sector.
- Lack of transparency and accountability in the private sector.
- Poor regulation of political contributions.
- Low public-sector wages.
- Weak enforcement of laws and regulations.
- Lack of free and independent media.
- Excessive discretionary authority of public officials.

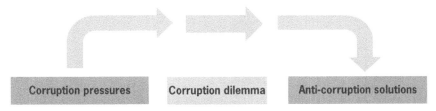

FIGURE 18.2 Dilemma of the Private Sector

Dilemma of the Private Sector

In a high-risk environment:

- How does one ensure that partners and competitors are ethical?
- How does one change the culture of doing business?
- How does one get competitors and stakeholders on board?

A key dilemma for companies seeking to combat corruption and build more competitive markets is: how do you engage your competitors? How do you engage those who feel that they do not have the resources to stand up to corruption (such as SMEs) or those who benefit from individual corrupt transactions? (See Figure 18.2.)

This is important because at the end of the day, as we established, to combat corruption you need to reform the environment within which companies operate and clean up individual transactions. You need to mobilize the business community.

Imagine yourself as a company that decides to stand up to corruption. If you are just one fish swimming against the current, without broader business support, can you be successful in reducing corruption, or will you fall a victim to it?

For multinationals operating in weak rule-of-law countries, there is a similar dilemma. Often, they may be held to a much higher standard, and it is difficult to compete on an equal footing with companies with weak governance or political protection and insider connections.

So how do you get the rest of the business community on board and ensure that your competitors as well are transparent and ethical?

Collective Action

Collective action usually involves multiple stakeholders (see Figure 18.3):

- Companies
- Civil society
- Government

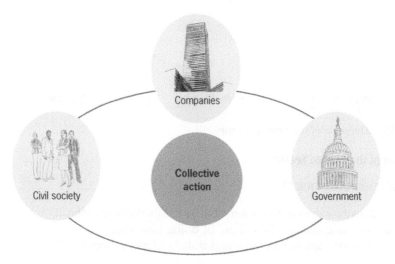

FIGURE 18.3 Collective Action Usually Involves Various Stakeholders

What we are talking about is trying to figure out how to make collective action work. The term *collective action* was popularized in politics, business, and economics by Mancur Olson, who began exploring a free-rider problem in business associations. Applied to the anti-corruption climate, the free-rider concept means that at the end of the day, each individual company will benefit from a more competitive, transparent climate, but few will be willing to individually invest their own resources or risk their own existence to achieve such a climate. A solution to solving this collective action problem is private incentives. If you can create incentives for companies to be more transparent, to be ethical, or to share resources (even in weak rule-of-law countries), you may begin to chip away at corruption.

Think about engaging the public sector, as well as various civil society organizations, in anti-corruption—as the field gets more complex and the number of stakeholders grows, it is much more difficult to develop and implement effective anti-corruption programs. Yet it does not mean it is impossible.

So how do we create those incentives and, more importantly, what are the tools that help companies solve the collective action problem and come together in the quest to reduce corruption and build a more competitive, predictable, and transparent business climate?

Different Types of Collective Action

There are different types of anti-corruption collective action programs, and while they all help achieve a common goal (lower levels of corruption),

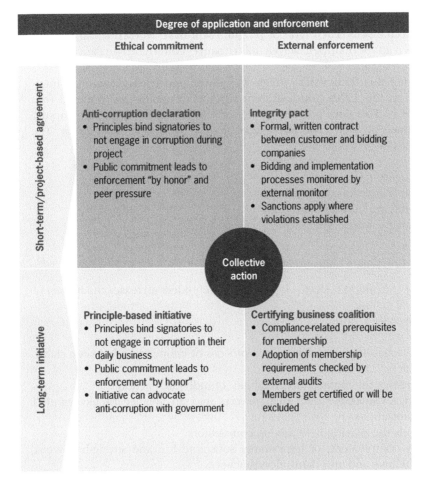

FIGURE 18.4 Characteristics of Collective Action

each works differently depending on the country environment, human and financial resources available, and so forth (see Figure 18.4).

More broadly, there is a difference between project- and transaction-based agreements and long-term initiatives. The difference is very intuitive; some efforts may seek to ensure that individual transactions are free of corruption, while more long-term initiatives seek to put in place institutions that will prevent overall corruption.

Within these two categories—short term and long term—we can also think about different types of programs. On the one hand, we have programs that are based on the ethical commitments of the participants; on

the other hand, we can also develop programs that have stricter enforcement mechanisms. Each type of program will have its own set of benefits
that have to be mapped across participants, country environments, and
so on.

Within this framework, which was developed by Transparency International in the 1990s, four different types of programs are outlined (see
Table 18.1). This does not mean others do not exist, but these four capture
the essence of what collective action against corruption is all about. The
four types of programs are:

1. Integrity pacts
2. Anti-corruption declarations
3. Certifying business coalitions
4. Principle-based initiatives

Fighting Corruption Collectively

Fighting corruption collectively with all stakeholders increases the impact of
individual action.

Collective action:

- Is a collaborative and sustained process of cooperation between stake-
  holders.
- Increases the impact and credibility of individual action.
- Brings vulnerable individual players into an alliance of like-minded
  organizations.
- Levels the playing field among competitors.
- May complement, or temporarily substitute for, and strengthen weak
  local laws and anti-corruption practices.

But collective action is not easy or quick, and requires patience, hard
work, and expertise.

All along, we have been discussing the business case for collective
action—why does it make sense for companies to engage with other stakeholders to reduce corruption? Overall, it makes sense because, simply put,
"companies cannot do it alone!"

Engaging in collective action provides a host of private benefits (incentives) to companies. Think about it as return on investment. You invest
time and resources, and in return, you not only reduce opportunities for
corruption, you also:

- Increase the impact and credibility of individual action.
- Level the playing field between competitors.

TABLE 18.1 Application and Objectives of Collective Action

Application	Objectives
Short-term **Integrity pacts**	• Preventive measure to reduce risk of corruption by increasing transparency of individual projects and business transactions • Create level playing field among bidding companies by external monitoring of processes • Provide consequences for corrupt behavior • Help protect participants from improper demands • Send a visible anti-corruption message to the public
Anti-corruption declarations	• Prevent corruption in individual projects and business transactions • Initiate open discussions on corruption • Collectively set individual behavior expectations • Reduce risk of corruption as bribe givers and takers realize that inappropriate behavior may be scrutinized • Create a signed statement that can be published and shared with subcontractors
Long-term **Certifying business coalitions**	• Promote standards of business conduct within certain country/sector • Signal to the public that members take measures to fight corruption • Position standards as a competitive advantage (e.g., certified members do not need to document their compliance measures in every tender) • Strengthen anti-corruption mechanisms
Principle-based initiatives	• Promote appropriate business conduct within certain country/sector • Leverage the voice of public, NGOs, religious bodies, and others to effectively address the problem of corruption • Join forces to push the government to implement anti-corruption laws (if country legal system does not yet have anti-corruption laws or if enforcement is weak)

- Improve the quality of legal and regulatory systems.
- Develop new markets for products and services.
- Introduce transparency and predictability in business transactions in emerging markets.

The point on transparency and predictability is particularly important. Time and time again, we see that while at certain points in time corruption may help resolve individual transactions, once it becomes institutionalized, companies suffer because it is impossible to predict how markets will work. In other words, in a corrupt environment, it is impossible to predict how a legislation will be enforced, who will make decisions, and why certain decisions will be made. How can you plan your business activities and decide on resource allocation and investment in such an environment?

Most importantly, collective action increases an individual company's impact by making fair business practices more common and elevating individual action or vulnerable individual players such as SMEs into an alliance of like-minded organizations. All stakeholders benefit from anti-corruption collective action, as follows:

Bidding Companies

- Increased chance of fair selection as a supplier and enhanced access to markets.
- Protection from legal penalties.
- Economization of finances formerly paid as bribes.
- Enhanced reputation.
- Assurance of ethically and responsibly behaved employees and competitors.

Customer

- Enhanced competition in bidding process—most efficient, not best-connected bidder wins bid.
- Enhanced reputation.
- Avoidance of time-consuming lawsuits/blocking points after decision on supplier company.
- Focus of business relationships on quality and reliability of goods and services.

Government

- Incentives are transparent.
- Strengthened rules of law, increased credibility, and political stability.
- Higher investment levels from domestic and foreign investors.
- Improved image of country.
- Effective governance mechanisms and more effective procurement.

Civil Society/Nongovernmental Organizations

- Improved access to essential resources, such as health care and education, and better social development if money/taxes are used for social projects instead of bribery.

- Increased trust and confidence in business.
- Consistent and fair enforcement of regulations.
- Greater traction of the objective of a more transparent environment and attention to corrupt practices.

At the end of the day, with proper programs in place, everyone benefits.

Bidding companies on major projects have an increased chance of fair selection as a supplier and enhanced access to markets. They also save money formerly paid as bribes.

Customers benefit from enhanced competition in the bidding process and avoid time-consuming lawsuits. Instead, they can focus on building business relationships and improving reliability of goods and services.

Civil society and nongovernmental organizations gain improved access to essential needs, such as health care and education. They also benefit from consistent and fair enforcement of regulations.

Governments strengthen rule of law and increase their own credibility, and can attract more investments from domestic and foreign investors.

Making It Come Together

The real benefit of collective action is the process by which the various initiatives come to fruition. This is why it is not enough to simply copy a law or a set of principles. When stakeholders come together, debate, discuss problems, and come up with solutions, they do more than develop an anti-corruption program. They also:

- Come up with local solutions to their own problems.
- Create a sense of ownership. This is very important—if stakeholders participate in developing the initiative themselves, if they invest their own resources, they have additional incentives to commit to it and see that it actually works.
- Build trust. Trust is particularly important in weak-rule-of-law countries, where institutions to reinforce transactions and enforce contracts are weak or missing altogether.

Collective action is by no means *the* solution to the corruption problem, but it is a very useful tool that has a successful track record of helping reduce corruption and building more competitive markets in emerging countries.

CHAPTER 19

Leveling the Playing Field

William P. Olsen

You have seen the term *leveling the playing field* used throughout this book. Unfortunately, a lot still needs to happen before this goal is attained. As globalization advances, business practices and accounting principles are becoming increasingly uniform. However, ethics continue to be local, deeply rooted in the culture. The importance of cultural differences is not confined to the problem of the different standards that underlie the "when in Rome" question that was also discussed, but also encompasses very different views of right and wrong. This requires us to understand the ways in which cultural differences are reflected in people's moral outlook.

Americans tend to be more legalistic and rule oriented. They tend not only to embody business ethics into laws that are rigorously enforced, but also to think of ethics as a set of rules for all to observe. Other cultures often view moral obligations as something arising out of specific relationships. Given the diversity of ethical outlooks around the world, it is going to take some time until common ground is found and some core standards can be agreed upon as part of the globalization process. Ultimately, the solution to many of these problems lies in the development of international agreements and codes of ethics. As guidelines for multinational companies become more detailed and comprehensive, business conduct may eventually become the same worldwide, and we will have achieved the level playing field that we desire. In the interim, there are some interesting theories out there that warrant some consideration by CEOs and business leaders while we wait for the emerging markets to adapt. First, from the book *The Integrity Advantage* by Adrian Gostick and Dana Telford, the authors set out to find the most ethical character traits by interviewing chief executive officers (CEOs) and business leaders who have acted with integrity throughout their careers; based on the interviews, the authors try to identify those characteristics that have set the CEOs and business leaders apart. They ultimately arrived at the conclusion that ethical business practices make good business sense in the long term. They identified the following 10 characteristics of high integrity:

1. You know that little things count.
2. You find the white (when others see gray).
3. You mess up, you 'fess up.
4. You create a culture of trust.
5. You keep your word.
6. You care about the greater good.
7. You act like you are being watched.
8. You are honest but modest.
9. You hire integrity.
10. You stay the course.

Also, throughout this book we have talked about policies, procedures, internal controls, laws, regulations, and ethical business practices. All of these aspects will help create a more ethical business environment; but imagine their impact if every CEO and board director also followed the simple steps listed here. Think of the corporate scandals of the past decade or so, and think about what could have happened if management had acted with integrity or the boards and others with oversight responsibilities had acted with responsibility once they became aware of the issues. Maybe there would still be an Arthur Andersen, WorldCom, and Lehman Brothers. The human factor is perhaps the greatest challenge to leveling the playing field in the global marketplace. Until management sets the right tone at the top and is willing to stay the course when others do not, we will continue fighting an uphill battle.

Another book for suggested reading is *Navigating the Badlands* by Mary O'Hara Devereaux. In her book, she identifies the challenges for U.S. organizations moving into the global marketplace. The book appropriately compares this process to the early settlers moving into the far western regions of the United States and the challenges that they faced. She lays out Eight Principles for Transformation into the new environment. They are as follows:

1. Scout for opportunities, but steer around the risks.
2. Act with integrity.
3. Seek diversity.
4. Learn rapidly.
5. Engage cultures.
6. Innovate radically.
7. Make decisions fast, but stay flexible.
8. Execute with discipline.

It is interesting how concepts like acting with integrity, avoiding risk, and executing with discipline keep showing up. If you apply these concepts to addressing the problem of global corruption, we come away with the following conclusions:

1. To be successful in the emerging market, we need to train and assign management that can identify the risks and steer organizations around the pitfalls of doing business in foreign lands. These individuals must always act with integrity while being innovative.
2. We need to embrace our diversity because it is our strength as we enter these new markets, and it may be the key to our success as we engage new cultures and try to find common ground in dealing with these issues.
3. Execute with discipline; the easy path is to go with the flow and do whatever everyone else is doing. That is not the trait of a leader, and if we are to change the tone, business leaders cannot take the path of least resistance.
4. We need to stay flexible because there will always be change and volatility in new markets.

Most importantly, businesses need to stay the course. As Ray Kroc, the founder of McDonald's Corporation, one of America's most successful and visible global companies, once said, "Persistence and persistence alone is omnipotent!"

Book Research Summary

Chapters 2 and 3

Hutchinson, Francis, Tom Laners, and Marie Wolkers. *The Global Corruption Barometer*. Berlin: Transparency International. December 9, 2005.

Langseth, Petter. *The United Nations Anti-Corruption Toolkit*. Vienna: Office of Foreign Ministry, 2001.

U.S. Department of State. *Fighting Global Corruption: Business Risk Management*. May 2001; www.dos.gov.

Chapter 3

Pieth, Mark. *Annual Report 2006*. The Working Group on Bribery, Office of Economic Cooperation and Development, 2006; www.oecd.org.

Chapter 4

The Economic Espionage Act, Anti-Kickback Act, Rackeeteer and Corrupt Organization Act, U.S. Criminal Code, Title 18; www.doj.gov.

Chapters 5 and 6

The Foreign Corrupt Practices Act. Department of Justice, U.S. Code, Title 15, Chapter 2B; www.doj.gov.

Chapter 14

"Auditors Can Help Detect and Deter Bribery and Kickbacks," Association of Certified Fraud Examiners, April 2003.

"Audit Those Vendors," Association of Certified Fraud Examiners, May/June 2003.

"Conducting Kickback Investigations," Association of Certified Fraud Examiners, July 2004.

"Construction Fraud," Association of Certified Fraud Examiners, May/June 2004.

"Fixing Prices and Rigging Bids," Association of Certified Fraud Examiners, July/August 2001.

"Mismanagement of Government Grant and Contract Funds," Association of Certified Fraud Examiners, November/December 2004.

National Procurement Fraud Task Force (NPFTF), www.usdoj.gov/criminal/npftf/

"Proactive Procurement Fraud Prevention Model," Fraud Prevention Services, 2002.

"Procurement and Fraud Remedies," Naval Inspector General, www.ig.navy.mil

"Procurement Fraud: How Tech Insiders Cheat Their Employers," www.baselinemag.com, June 7, 2006.

"Report to the Nation," Association of Certified Fraud Examiners, 2008.

Chapter 19

Boatright, John R. *Ethics and the Conduct of Business*. Upper Saddle River, NJ: Prentice Hall, 2003.

Devereaux, Mary O'Hara. *Navigating the Badlands: Thriving in the Decade of Radical Transformation*. San Francisco: Jossey-Bass, 2004.

Gostick, Adrian, and Dana Telford. *The Integrity Advantage: How Taking the High Road Creates a Competitive Advantage in Business*. Layton, UT: Gibbs Smith, 2003.

Grant Thornton Publications

Baskin, Dorsey, and Bill Olsen. "Under the Magnifying Glass: Special Investigations." *Currency*, March 2009.

Olsen, Bill. "Anti-Money Laundering and Financial Institutions." *Currency*, Summer 2005.

Olsen, Bill. "Corporate Governance: A Key to Unmasking Fraudulent Activity." *Currency*, Winter 2003.

Side bar article: "Blowing the Whistle on Corporate Fraud."

Olsen, William P., Richard Kirt West, Nancy R. Grunberg, and Danette R. Edwards. "Navigating the Perils of FCPA Investigations in Emerging Markets." GT white paper, January 2009.

Preber, Brad, and Trent Gazzaway. "Hear That Whistle Blowing! Establishing an Effective Complaint-Handling Process." *CorporateGovernor* white paper, August 2006 (updated May 2009).

Olsen, Bill. "Save, Toss, Recycle? Companies Struggle to Find the Right Document Retention Policy." *CorporateGovernor*, Spring 2004.

Outside Publications

"Corruption: Why It Matters." U.S. Department of Justice, 2001. Appendix A, FCPA Antibribery Provisions.

"Federal Sentencing Guidelines." Ethics Resource Center, January 31, 2002.

Olsen, Bill. "Don't Crimp." *FEI Magazine,* January/February 2007. Reprinted with permission from *Financial Executive.* © by Financial Executives International; 973.765.1000; www.financialexecutives. org.

Olsen, Bill, Sterl Greenhalph, and Djordjija Petkoski. "Business Case for Collective Action against Corruption." June 2008. Reprinted with permission from the World Bank Institute. © by The World Bank Group; www.fightingcorruption.org; contact fightcorruption@ worldbank.org.

Ramamoorti, Sri, and Bill Olsen, "Fraud: The Human Factor." *FEI Magazine,* July/August 2007. Reprinted with permission from *Financial Executive,* © by Financial Executives International; 973.765.1000; www.financialexecutives.org.

"Racketeer Influenced and Corrupt Organizations Act"; www.usdoj.gov.

Other articles within this Word document:

"Anti-Kickback Act of 1986." U.S. Department of Justice, www. usdoj.gov/usao/eousa/foia_reading_room/usam/title9/crm00927 .htm.

"Economic Espionage Act of 1996." Wikipedia; http://en. wikipedia.org/wiki/Economic_Espionage_Act_of_1996.

"Price Fixing, Bid Rigging, and Market Allocation Schemes: What They Are and What to Look For: An Antitrust Primer." U.S. Department of Justice, 2003; www.usdoj.gov/atr/ public/guidelines/primer-ncu.htm.

"Promoting Good Business Practices in Transitional Economies." U.S. Department of Justice, 2003.

Index

Printed and bound by CPI Group (UK) Ltd, Croydon, CR0 4YY

23/04/2025

14661005-0001